The Robinson Memoirs

HOW BIG
Is Your *God?*

Trust this will be an encouragement to you.

C. Robinson
Terry Robinson
II Cor 4:7

Connie
ROBINSON

HOW BIG IS YOUR GOD?

Unless otherwise indicated, all Scripture quotations are taken from the Holy Bible, King James Version, which is in the public domain.

ISBN: 978-1-77069-374-6

Printed in Canada.

Word Alive Press
131 Cordite Road, Winnipeg, MB R3W 1S1
www.wordalivepress.ca

This book is our memoirs of God's work and dealings in our lives. Names, places, and incidents are related as accurately as our memory files and hard copy records can produce. Any resemblance to actual events, organizations or persons living or dead is entirely intentional.

A special thanks to our daughter Jaclyn who bravely agreed to help with editing.

CONTENTS

FOREWORD

How Big Is Your God?

It had just happened again. In fact, that was the second time in a couple of months. This time it was out at a missionary conference at Millar College of the Bible in Saskatchewan. Someone from the past came up to Jerry and said, "You know how I remember you? HOW BIG IS YOUR GOD?" She went on to share about the ministry God had led her into after college. After listening to her story, Jerry asked her, "IS HE BIG ENOUGH?" And she said with conviction, "YES, HE IS BIG ENOUGH!"

When Jerry got home and told me that story, I said, "Maybe that was your one pivotal message in life that God wanted you to share with people." Come to think of it, I guess that concept really is pivotal in life. Without that deep, personal conviction, we live our lives on a different plane.

I remember the agonizing Jerry did, preparing for his annual recruiting tour to various colleges. At that particular time, he was recruiting staff for Camp Chestermere. How does a man who struggles with dyslexia and all its challenges—spelling, reading, recalling, flipping letters and numbers—find public speaking anything less than terrifying? How does a man who feels out of sync with the academic world face addressing college students with confidence? How does a man, short of stature, and with a unique voice that no one forgets, look forward to challenging audiences of up to 700 students?

Each year it was not an assignment to be desired! Jerry would spend hours and hours, both day and night, on his face before God, beseeching God for His message. Jerry already knew he was not going to impress anyone with his own words! That year, 1983, as he stood before the students, he paused; and then, in a drawn out shout, he asked several times, "HOW…BIG…IS…YOUR…GOD? IS…HE…BIG…ENOUGH?" He went on to recount some of the stories and miracles that God had done at Camp Chestermere and in other ministry settings. It stuck. Almost 30 years later, people still remember.

Through all the ups and downs of our lives, we have been challenged ourselves with the same words. How hard it is to keep perspective! How wonderful when we do! As you read these pages, may you be encouraged to believe a God who really is big enough for all the chapters of life.

1

GOD SWAYS THE VOTE

It was the WORST possible timing! The phone was ringing in the office. "Oh, not now, Lord!" thought Jerry.

Jerry was at a Camp Chestermere board meeting, and the chairman had just called for a vote on the motion at hand. As the director, Jerry had been presenting a challenge for the camp. That year, 1980, was the camp's 25th anniversary. There were lots of facility repairs and upgrades needing attention; and, with the growing camp outreach, it was time to address them. Jerry was putting out a challenge to the board in the 25th anniversary year to raise $25,000 over and above general giving to cover the urgent repairs. The verse God had impressed him with was from Hebrews 11:6 *"But without faith it is impossible to please him: for he* that cometh to God must believe that he is, and that he is a rewarder of them that diligently seek him."

The motion had been made, and the discussion had gone on for some time. While the needs were obvious, the fund raising target just seemed unrealistic. The pros and cons were aired. Jerry could read the atmosphere—it was not going well. The chairman wanted to push on to the other items of business, and so he called for a vote on the anniversary project. Just then the phone rang.

The secretary went to answer and came back to call Jerry to the phone.

"Get a number and tell them I'll call back," he said. There was no way he wanted to miss getting in his vote on the motion.

"But the man is calling from the Calgary airport," she explained. "He's just on his way through and needs to talk with you *now* before his plane leaves."

With great reluctance, Jerry excused himself and headed to the phone. "Don't vote till I get back," he called over his shoulder.

The man on the phone was John, a fellow who had attended a little Bible study we had held back in 1975. John and his wife were new Christians at that time, but we had lost touch with them during the last few years. He was in the oil business and was away a lot. Jerry was very surprised to hear his voice.

John quickly brought him up to date. He had just recently finished a contract job in the Middle East. Since he had completed the work a year earlier than expected, besides receiving an excellent wage, he had also been given a big bonus. He said that he and his wife had been lying in bed in Houston, Texas the night before, discussing how to minimize some tax implications. They both came up with an idea. Why not make a donation to that camp Jerry was working at!

Since John was flying through Calgary the next day, he decided to call from the airport. "Your camp wouldn't be able to use $30,000 would it?" he asked.

Wow! When Jerry went back to the board meeting, he said, "We don't really need your vote. God just raised the money." When he told them what had transpired on the phone call, no one could believe it. "I knew you wouldn't," said Jerry, "so I wrote down his phone number at the airport. I've got it right here on my hand. He's waiting for you to call him back to confirm it."

Incredulous, the chairman went to the phone and called. He came back with a sheepish grin. "Yes, the man says as soon as he gets the money out of his Swiss bank account, we'll have the $30,000."

That night, the board voted to pass the motion about seeking to raise the extra $25,000. And guess what! During that year, more than $27,500 in additional project funds came in, not even counting the oilman's gift.

And that phone call—the BEST possible timing—God's timing! How big is your God?

2

GROWING UP

Two Backgrounds

Thinking back to our childhood years, it was obvious that God had shaped the circumstances of our early lives to begin teaching us about our big God and what it meant to follow His ways. He was uniquely preparing us for what was ahead.

From the outset, Jerry had to be a fighter! He was born March 17, 1945 in Vulcan, Alberta, seven weeks premature. He was an identical twin, and together the babies weighed about six pounds. There was only one incubator available. Since Jerry was the smaller twin, he won the incubator. At first neither twin was expected to live, so the nurses just called the babies Pat and Mike in honor of their Irish birth date. Mother Inez Robinson rescued them with official names, Gerald Daniel Robinson and Harold Michael Robinson. Harold did not make it past three days: Gerald did. Years later, Mom Robinson said she thought she knew why God took one baby home early. He knew she could not have handled two like Gerald. It seemed that he was either just getting into trouble, or just coming out of trouble!

It was in school, when there were several "Geralds," that he first started to be called "Jerry." Besides, he found he could make better "J's" than "G's".

The concerning factor was that his name meant "mighty warrior." And I guess he really tried to live up to it. An early picture captures him pinching another little boy. On one of the first days of school, he walked up to the teacher, punched her in the stomach, and walked home. He was always an advocate for the underdog, and although small of stature, he soon had a reputation. In fact, his teacher gave him "special" jobs to do after school—so the rest of the kids could get home unscathed. Of course his tough front did not stop him from fainting dead away after school immunization shots.

And there were apparently some interesting hospital experiences growing up. He had to have his tonsils removed as a child, and was anxious to go home. The hospital staff encouraged him that it would be just one more sleep before it was time to leave the hospital. We're not quite sure what was going on in his mind that day. It could be that he had a little nap; and when he woke up, he thought it was the next day. Or it could be he just decided he wanted to go home. Whatever his reasoning, he chose to take matters into his own hand, and off he started. As he headed past the nursing station, someone happened to look up and exclaim, "There goes a patient!" By the time they reached him, he was out the front door and heading down the steps on his way home, with his hospital gown flapping open in the breeze behind him.

The next episode happened in his teens when he again landed in hospital for some minor surgery. He was absolutely not impressed when a young female candy striper (a hospital volunteer designated by distinctive red and white striped uniform) arrived to give him a sponge bath. Maybe that explains his inclination to avoid hospitals entirely by trying to cure everything with Pepto Bismal!

I arrived late by several days, coming inconveniently on December 24, 1948. You can imagine how "special" my birthday celebrations were each year, happening on Christmas Eve! It was unique, though, to share my birth date with my Grandma Cornell, and also an aunt. Actually, in order to avoid the Christmas overload, my birthday was usually celebrated on December 16 which was the birth date of my older sister, Marilyn. I didn't mind getting my presents early!

Our home was right down town Calgary—5th Avenue and 8th Street—before any of the high-rises. We even had grass boulevards on our block. Our home was tall and skinny, but not very big. For a while we had three rental units in the house besides our main floor home. German immigrants occupied a basement studio apartment, a cousin boarded in another basement bedroom, and a family friend rented the apartment on the second floor.

My sister and I shared the tiny back bedroom with bunk beds. We used to race getting dressed in the morning. I had a ridiculous garter belt to hold up my long stockings. Mom had added shoulder straps so it would not fall off my skinny frame. Each morning it seemed to take fiendish delight in being hopelessly tangled. I would get so frustrated and upset, trying to sort it out, that I usually ended up with a spanking instead of the winner's bragging rights. My Dad just did not appreciate my temper tantrums or care about the unfair advantage my sister had. Oh for panty hose or leotards back then!

I did not go to kindergarten, but when I was 5 ½ years old, I started Grade 1 at McDougall School, just a block away. I loved school. My Mom taught a Bible club there after school, so I was off to a good start. All the teachers knew who I was, and I set out to be "teacher's pet" in every grade.

For sure it must have worked in Grade 1. The Board of Education was experimenting with accelerating students who did well in citywide tests. I border-lined the tests. But right after taking the tests, I came down with mumps, or measles, or one of those other horrific childhood ailments. The teacher vouched for me, saying that she was sure I would have easily passed if I had been feeling a hundred percent. So, on the basis of her recommendations, I was accelerated. That meant taking three grades in two years. And she was right. I had no problem academically all through school. I was top of my class.

Socially was another story. Here I was, now a year and a half younger than lots of the kids in my grade. And I was skinny, short, and late developing. I remember being embarrassed the first day of Grade 10 at Central High, a high school noted for its academic prowess. Each student was to answer to his or her name. We were also asked to state our age. When I said, "thirteen", everybody turned around and stared. Of course in Sunday School, divisions went by ages, so I was back with kids who were a grade or two beneath me at school. It seemed I didn't fit anywhere. Thankfully, God provided one or two close friends I could hang out with in each school grade—and it was great to be finished high school at sixteen.

School was an interesting experience for Jerry. In fact his teacher's comments on his report card stated, "Jerry just doesn't seem to understand what school is all about." At the end of his first year, his teacher concluded that Jerry should be a "leader" in his class the next year—again in Grade 1.

His big struggle was with reading. When he started Grade 1 in Alberta, the educators were just experimenting with teaching kids to read by pictures. Then he moved to Jamestown, North Dakota where the kids had already learned phonics. As a result, he missed phonics. Compounded by dyslexia challenges, reading was not his strength. When the class was asked to read orally, he was busy counting down the rows and down the pages to figure out what his lines would be. It was awful.

Although reading was not his forte, he seemed to have great success with the ladies! In First Grade in Jamestown, he began walking a girl home from school. That was just the start of a long chain of female friends until Bible school.

He also got to know the school principal well. He says they were on a first-name basis. In fact, he got to take classes from the principal—at a desk pulled right up beside the principal's desk. Mom Robinson actually acknowledges that some of Jerry's teachers were rather interesting individuals, and Jerry's troubles at school were not entirely his fault.

Occasionally, even the police got into the action—like the time when Jerry was just a boy and had decided to run away from home. After packing his suitcase and heading off down the block, he circled back to carefully remove a couple bricks and squeeze under his own front porch, pulling in the bricks behind him. It was a great location from which to listen to all the action of those searching for the missing kid.

And then there was the time the doorbell rang early in the morning and the police asked Dad Robinson if he had a son named Gerald.

"Yes," said his dad.

"Do you know where he is?" was the next question.

"Well, of course, he's in bed!" But when Dad went to get him, he was shocked to discover Jerry was really sitting in the back seat of the police cruiser. Jerry and his friends had been out rolling garbage cans down a hill to celebrate Halloween. A neighbor caught Jerry by the ear and held him until the police arrived. As the son of a Baptist pastor, Jerry was a little concerned for the family reputation and how the rumors would spread about him sitting in the police station overnight!

Now sports…that was a real highlight! Jerry was athletically inclined, and a natural competitor. But there was the problem of size. At 5' 4" and 118 lbs., Jerry could not really consider basketball and football as promising options. Since his mother refused to sign a permission slip for him to participate in boxing, the sports of choice were track and field, cross-country, and Olympic-style wrestling. And he did very well—going to State finals in three sports. We still have the newspaper clippings from those days.

I was not quite three when I was asked to sing "Star of the East" as a solo at the Sunday School Christmas program. Wow! Why me? Maybe it had something to do with the fact that Mom sang solos for several weddings, or that people used to turn around and wonder who that kid was that was singing so heartily in church behind them. Or maybe it was just that the Christmas program committee's first choice of soloist was not available. At any rate, Mom worked with me at home to learn all the words. I still remember that day when it was my turn to sing "Star of the East" during the concert. I absolutely refused to look at Mom who was sitting in a front row mouthing all the words. I didn't need her help. I knew them!

My sister and I were taught to sing duets—Mom played for us—and I guess we were a bit of a novelty because we were asked to sing at many functions: church services, radio broadcasts, special events, and lots of weddings. I was so happy when I was six and was asked to be a flower girl at a wedding. Finally, my matching dress was longer than my sister's when we sang at that reception.

Later, in my teens, I formed a trio with a cousin and another church friend. For three years we practiced lots and sang frequently. Excellence was important. But I was not very sensitive to my sister during that time. She did not have quite as good an ear for music, so if invitations came to sing, I would offer my trio instead of singing a duet with Marilyn. Years later I had to go and apologize to my sister for forgetting I Corinthians 13:1 (Robinson version) *"Though I 'sing' with the tongues of men and of angels, and have not charity, I am become as sounding brass, or a tinkling cymbal."*

Piano lessons were also part of everyday life growing up. My piano teacher tried to assign me different music than Marilyn had learned because, if I had heard it, I would play it by ear instead of reading the music. It was fun to work out choruses and piano arrangements on the piano. I am grateful for Bun Shatto, an uncle of Jerry's, who led our Junior Department in Sunday School. He got two or three of us who were taking piano lessons to take turns playing for the open session. That was my start. Later, I was asked to play for Sunday services. I liked accompanying much better than when I felt that everyone was just listening to me, like when I had to play for offertories. I continued with piano lessons until achieving Grade 10 in Royal Conservatory, but decided not to take an additional year or two to complete the music degree. I was not planning to teach piano as a career. Later, when we lived in Abbotsford for a couple years, the church paid for me to take ten lessons on the organ with Roy Morden, a crusade organist. I felt honored. Those lessons were invaluable in transitioning from piano to church organ playing.

It was several years later that some former Bible school classmates called and asked if we were interested in their Hammond organ since it was just sitting idle. We had no money for that kind of purchase so we turned it down. After a few weeks, they called again with an ultimatum. "If you want that organ, come and get it for free and get it out of here." We did! What a big God to provide something like that!

Jerry took piano lessons, too, until his teacher called his mother and suggested she could use her money more wisely. A finger injury in football sidelined even his clarinet playing in the high-school band. It is hard to cover the holes with a finger that no longer bends at the first joint.

Almost without exception, everyone made the college choir in Bible school. Well, almost! Bill Anderson, our choir director, had Jerry sing a line in audition like everyone else. "Thank you, that's enough!" he stated, with his eyebrows going up and down conversely. It wasn't that Jerry sang off key. It was just that his range was limited, and he had no idea if he was singing melody or harmony. If the melody line got past his range, he would flip to harmony.

Who would have guessed that, in the future, he would lead large audiences of children in music? He could really get them to sing. And who would have guessed he would one day get invited to be the choir director for a Mennonite choir?

That blunder began one summer when Jerry had agreed that our family would be responsible for leading the worship music for a summer service. He was counting on our kids to sing, play guitar, and generally carry the worship time, forgetting that they were scattered that summer—some at camp, some elsewhere. When the Sunday approached, I reminded him we were on for music. I said I would be playing the piano, so that left him leading the worship. He chose some familiar hymns and choruses, got up, and waved his arms like a pro; and the people sang—really sang!

A couple weeks later, I got a phone call from Al, one of the leaders in the church. Jerry was not home, so Al told me what was on his mind. The people had apparently really enjoyed Jerry's song leading. In fact, they were still talking about it. Al said they were losing their choir director that fall, and asked if Jerry would consider the position. I was very polite and very non-committal, but I was almost rolling on the floor laughing. I discretely said I would have Jerry call Al when he got back home.

When Jerry called and heard what Al wanted, he was shocked. Instantly his mind was in overdrive, wondering what he could say to get out of this situation. He began to protest with, "I have to be away a lot with our work."

"Oh, we've thought about that," said Al. "We can get a substitute for the times you have to be gone."

Now it was time for the stark truth. "Al," he said," I can't tell a black note from a white note. I'm definitely not the man you want." So Jerry declined the choir conductor position, but he still leads congregational songs occasionally. So much for Bill Anderson's evaluation!

My life, growing up, was in nice neat little packages. I had a conventional family, lived in the same house, and attended the same church. My dad had the same job teaching at Berean Bible College all those years, and my mom was at home caring for us. I went to school, took piano lessons, attended Pioneer Girls Club, and later Young Peoples and Youth for Christ. Summers were spent out at Camp Chestermere and going on family camping trips. Life was stable and predictable.

In contrast, Jerry's life had variety. His dad, as a pastor, moved to different churches. After pastoring in Longview and Wainwright, Alberta, and traveling overseas with Youth for Christ, he accepted a church in Jamestown, North Dakota. Most of Jerry's grade school happened there.

Now pastors' kids are supposed to be well behaved — models of excellent deportment. For Jerry, that was tough to live up to. Occasionally Dad Robinson would have to ask one of the prominent church ladies, Mrs. Storehog, to come and sit by "those boys that are misbehaving in the front row." Once he even had Jerry come and sit up on the platform in one of the big fancy chairs right behind him. It didn't take Jerry long to discover that if he just barely lifted off the seat, the cushioned seat would fill with air. Then, when he sat back down, the air would swoosh out of the air vents on the sides of the padding. That was great entertainment during the rest of the sermon—for everyone but his dad.

Just before Jerry entered High School, his dad accepted a church in Wausau, Wisconsin. That summer, Jerry worked in Alberta with his uncles. At the end of the summer, before taking the bus down to Wisconsin, Jerry thought he had better get a haircut.

Now the barber and Jerry had a little history. Usually Grandma Shatto cut Jerry's hair when the family came up from the States for vacation. One time, however, a friend and Jerry had gone to this barber for haircuts. Somehow, on a dare, they both decided to get Mohawk haircuts. Jerry went first—and then the friend backed out. When the boys returned home, Jerry's dad took one look at the new haircut and…well…the friend fled. The strong admonition from Dad was to never get another haircut like that!

Jerry had not been back to that barbershop until now. And, sure enough, there was the same barber, still cutting hair. Jerry asked, "Did you ever give anyone a Mohawk haircut?"

"Yes," said the barber. Once I gave a black boy a Mohawk, and another time there were two boys that came in and wanted them, but I only did one of them."

Jerry said, "I was that boy."

"You wouldn't want another one, would you?" grinned the barber.

"Uh…sure!" said Jerry.

So without any premeditation, it happened again.

Next came the bus ride home from Calgary to Wisconsin, and you can well imagine that nobody wanted to sit beside him! And then came the Sunday morning taxi ride to Immanuel Baptist Church, where the worship service was already underway. This was a new town, and Jerry had never been there before. Jerry quietly entered the Baptist church and slipped into a back seat. There was just one problem. The seats were like old theatre seats, and as Jerry pushed the seat down, it squawked. Every eye turned and almost in unison, the mouths flew open. There were muted gasps. And from the pulpit Jerry's dad said, "I'd like you to meet my oldest son, Gerald." That was Jerry's grand entrance to a church which has faithfully supported our ministry for over forty years. We still hear the story of his Mohawk haircut when we go back there to visit.

In both of our homes, the gospel message was clearly taught. I cannot tell you the date I became a Christian. I remember inviting the Lord Jesus to forgive my sin and come into my life several different times. On one of those occasions, I was bent over the sink while my mother washed my hair. I'm not sure if I thought she was going to drown me, or what prompted me to be concerned about my eternal destiny at that moment. Often I would lay in bed at night with tears running down my face, thinking about the crucifixion scene and what it meant. I knew that I was a sinner and deserved eternal punishment in hell. I knew God loved me, and that He had sent His own perfect son, the Lord Jesus Christ to take my punishment on the cross. I knew Jesus poured out His life's blood for me, and that Jesus' resurrection proved the price was paid. My part was to believe it, and accept it for myself. Then, one day, the truths of John 10:27–30 and 1 John 5:11–13 suddenly became real to me. I didn't have to keep asking over and over. It was settled! God does not lie, and He would keep His Word! What a wonderful assurance.

Jerry was just a little boy when, one night, as his mother tucked him into bed and went to turn out the light, he called out, "Don't turn off the light. I'm the lost lamb." Over his bed was a picture of Jesus, the Good Shepherd, reaching down to pick up a lost lamb. That night, Mom Robinson carefully explained again to Jerry what it meant to ask Jesus to be the Savior for his sin. And that night, as Jerry recalls, was the night he prayed to receive Christ. All through his growing up years, in spite of his mischievousness, Jerry had a soft heart for God. In high school he helped adult sponsors plan events and programs for the junior highs. And as he graduated from school and considered his future, he knew there was something he had to take care of—a promise he had made to his folks.

3

Becoming Doers, Not Hearers Only

Bible School Years

August 1965–September 1968

Jerry's parents wanted all their children to attend at least one year of Bible school. When Jerry reached that point, he had some interesting viable options other than attending Bible school. With his athletic skills, he had been offered scholarships for college in the States. He had already taken some training at the Wausau Technical Institute, had a good job, and was eligible to be drafted into the US Army. But, there was the matter of the promise he'd made. Since he had promised his folks he would take one year of Bible school, he figured he might as well get it over with. His older sister, Loretta, had gone to Moody Bible Institute. But since Jerry had already worked in Alberta for a summer or two with his uncles, he opted to apply to Berean Bible College in Calgary.

It was only by God's grace that Jerry ever made it. The one concern was that his reputation had preceded him, and the staff was a little apprehensive about this young man wanting to come from Wausau, Wisconsin. It was somewhat reassuring, though, that the Bible school staff knew his family connections. His dad, Rev. George Robinson had served with Youth for Christ early in his ministry, traveled around the world, been on radio in Calgary with Bob Simpson and The Sunrise Gospel Hour, pastored in Alberta, North Dakota, and Wisconsin. His granddad, Roscoe Shatto, had even served on the board for Berean Bible College. His uncle, Bun Shatto, had helped dig the foundations for Mayland Heights Baptist Church—later called Crossroads Community Church, and had helped create the island on the lake shore out at Camp Chestermere.

There were other connections, too. My dad, Rev. Arthur Cornell, was then serving as the principal at Berean. Back when Dad had attended Prophetic Bible Institute, the forerunner of Berean, many students had gone out on ministry teams to the rural areas. Dad had stayed in the Roscoe Shatto home (Jerry's grandparents) down by Arrowwood. That had been an interesting experience, enduring the pranks of the Shatto boys. Once, after Dad just finished polishing his car, Don Shatto artistically added mud faces to the surface. Dad was not impressed! At least Dad figured their daughter, Inez, might be more congenial. Apparently one time when Dad was heading over to Gleichen to hold a service, he asked Inez (who later became Mrs. George Robinson and Jerry's mother) to come along to play piano. She was suspicious of Dad's intentions and chose to decline. So, there was some interesting history between our two families although Jerry and I knew nothing of each other.

In spite of any reservations the college administration might have had about Jerry's past, he was officially accepted by Berean Bible College. After all, everyone deserves a chance. So, in the fall of 1965, on a day pouring the rain, Jerry loaded up his little 1959 MGA white sports car and headed off on the 1370 miles to Alberta.

Shortly after arriving, Jerry's Uncle Bun Shatto invited Jerry over for dinner. During the course of the conversation, Uncle Bun asked Jerry if there were any good-looking girls at Bible College.

"Yes," said Jerry, "there are a few."

Bun Shatto's twin daughters and I had attended church and camp together, but there was a little coolness in our relationship. The twins also sang together. Over the years there had been some incidents between the twins and the Cornell sisters, (especially me) over singing and camp boyfriends. Then there was the time when the twins were counseling at Camp Chestermere, and had sneaked out late at night with some others to go to the Calgary Stampede. When word got back to my dad, the camp director, somehow I was suspected for spilling the beans, and rightfully so. Needless to say, Jerry had already been warned by his twin cousins to avoid the Cornell girls.

Uncle Bun, wanting to get Jerry off to a good start, told Jerry he had a special assignment for him. He was to look over all the girls at college, pick out the ugliest one, and write her name in ink on his hand. "Now make sure she is the ugliest," he reiterated.

Two weeks passed, and Jerry was invited back to Uncle Bun's. After dinner, Uncle Bun asked Jerry if he had picked out the ugliest. "Yes, I think I've found her," he answered.

"Well," said Uncle Bun, "when she begins to look nice to you, that's the sign you've been at Bible school too long and it's time to get out of there." And so, with that profound advice, Bible School years began. However, the girl Jerry had picked out didn't last more than a month at school. And it wasn't me!

During the first couple weeks of college, I was not in class, but was helping with the harvest at Bill Anderson's farm east of Langdon. He farmed in the summer and taught music at Berean in the winter. In fact, it was during harvest one year, that I did my first driving—a one-ton pick-up out in the field. It was not until later that I learned I had made an early impression on Jerry by my absence! During roll call, Jerry kept noticing the empty desk beside him. When I did arrive, Jerry noticed something else. We happened to have the very same Bibles—Scofield Reference Bibles. I guess he had heard that I was a good student, so when I marked something in my Bible, he marked it in his Bible. When I wrote something down, he wrote something down. He claims it was just not fair that when the tests came back, I would get over 100% (bonus question scores added), and he was happy to pass! He stretches that story a bit! He actually did pretty well with his grades, but really had to work at it with the learning challenges of dyslexia.

I didn't stay in the college dorm since I was spending about three hours a day practicing piano. It would have been difficult to get that much practice time in with the limited music practice rooms at college. Each morning, when I arrived at school with Dad, I would leave my books in the classroom, and wander off till it was time for class to begin. I'd often return to discover my books rearranged on several other desks, thanks to Jerry. He was full of mischief. We became friends, but it wasn't until spring of 1966 that we began to date.

There was good reason for Jerry to be awarded a jolly jumper at the student Christmas party for being involved in the most pranks, and getting away with it. There was the ingenious bugging of the inter-dorm phone—the wires of which just happened to pass through Jerry's dorm room closet. It was great entertainment, eavesdropping on all the romantic conversations between the guys and the girls. There was the time when absolutely everything was removed from one of the guy's dorm rooms so when he returned late at night, even the light bulb was gone. The poor fellow kept looking at the door number, and then the empty room inside. When he trudged off down the hall to report the event to the men's dean, the guys sprang into action, completely replacing everything before the dean arrived. Well… the pictures were still swinging a bit. And there was the time during a fall missionary conference when there was the occasional "Amen" or "Hallelujah." However, the true meaning for "Amen" was when Calgary scored in the football game that was being discreetly monitored with earphones.

During the summer after the first year, Jerry worked in road construction for his uncles, twinning the No. 1 Highway by Pense and Balgonie in Saskatchewan. The working conditions were pretty rough with the crew guys, especially in the bunkhouse. But the pay was great. He went back to Bible School in the fall with a healthy account. However by spring, it had dwindled to almost nothing. It was as if he had holes in his pockets. Once his little MGA sports car just coasted up to the gas pumps—absolutely empty. He asked for 25 cents worth of gas—that's all he had. Of course back then that was enough for about one gallon of gas. He didn't even have enough to pay for the insurance on his car until he got an anonymous gift of $30 along with a brief note that was signed "I. L.Y." It was not till some time later that he finally learned what the initials stood for—"I Love You." The gift was from me, and I was not very happy when I learned that he had given some of the money to his roommate whom I had briefly dated in the first year.

By the end of the second year, the impact of Bible school was changing Jerry's priorities. From the very outset, Jerry had put his name in for practical work—preaching at street meetings, being involved in a children's Bible club at Ramsay School, helping at the Third Street East Mission, and teaching Sunday School out at Hope Chapel in Bowness. Now he was beginning to think, not just of earning money during the summer months, but also of how God might use him.

About that time, Betsy Theaker, of Child Evangelism Fellowship® (CEF) in Ontario, came to speak at Berean, recruiting summer missionaries. She stayed about a week. Each day she encouraged students to come and talk with her about teaching 5-Day Clubs® in Ontario. Each day, Jerry thought about it... and did not go. Finally on the last day, he went to her room and knocked. She was packing up to leave, but immediately set her stuff down and invited Jerry in to chat. She encouraged him to fill out an application form, saying that it did not commit him. I wonder if she had any idea that that was the beginning of a lifetime commitment to ministry with children!

That first summer with CEF of Ontario in 1967 was a huge learning curve. After two weeks of intensive training, Jerry was sent out to advertise from house to house, and then to teach four clubs each day for a week, staying with different host families in each community. Saturdays were travel days, and then on Sundays he would give his testimony and share reports in the next church. They were busy weeks, and through them Jerry was stirred with the needs and the responses from boys and girls. What a thrill to counsel boys and girls and lead them to Christ. And Jerry was touched that God could even use him!

But the pay—well, he earned $10 a week for 10 weeks. That was just the amount needed to cover re-registration for school that fall. When he arrived back at Bible college for his final year, he told the Lord that whenever his account was empty, he would leave Bible school. An amazing thing happened. All that winter, God supplied through various jobs, and gifts. Sometimes donors would request their gift go towards someone who had done Christian work the previous summer. At the end of the year, Jerry still had money in his account. And he had even run his car the whole winter!

Well, if God could do that, Jerry decided that after graduation he would teach 5-Day Clubs for another summer—this time in Alberta. Since CEF of Alberta was not provincially organized at that time, all the summer missionaries traveled to Regina, Saskatchewan for training before returning to Alberta to teach. It was another great summer of outreach; and while in the Calgary area, he stayed at Berean. Too soon it was over. What next?

By summer's end, Jerry still did not know. He needed some answers. Frankly, at that point, he was ready for any answer! Jerry was at a crossroads in life—one of many, as life unfolded. But this was getting urgent! Students for Berean Bible College would soon be arriving. He was no longer one of them. He needed to be leaving, but to what? What was next? Why didn't God tell him?

Something had been eating away at Jerry about the options ahead. There was one thing he determined never to be, and that was a pastor. Having been raised in a pastor's home, Jerry had witnessed first-hand the stresses, the workload, the sermon preparation, the expectations, and the hassles that go with that role. It was not for him! But as Jerry kept praying about his future, he finally came to the point of yielding to God that resistance to becoming a pastor. He even sent out applications to two or three country churches that needed youth pastors. But still nothing.

And then the phone rang. It was Dave Chapman, the CEF provincial director for Saskatchewan. He had met Jerry at the beginning of that summer at the Regina training. He said they were looking for an area director for western Saskatchewan and asked if Jerry would consider it?

Meanwhile, Jerry's uncles were offering Jerry work with them. Jerry was confused and went to talk with his Grandpa Shatto. "Well," said his Grandpa thoughtfully, "anybody can drive a cat or a buggy in road construction, but not just anybody can go lead children to Christ."

But if Jerry was really going to accept the Saskatchewan CEF invitation, so many things had to come together fast! For starters, an MGA sports car was not exactly ideal for Saskatchewan winters. That same day, a former fellow student showed up at Berean and asked Jerry if he had ever considered selling his car. Wow! They agreed on a price of $500, and one roadblock was down.

Then Jerry headed off to the barbershop to get a needed haircut—thankfully, not another Mohawk! In the next chair just happened to be my pastor, Bill Laing. They got talking about Jerry's plans; and Pastor Laing said, "I'm travelling to Saskatoon in a few days with an empty station wagon. You could come along and take all your stuff." Amazing! That was exactly where Jerry was to head, since the Saskatchewan CEF staff was having some meetings there. What a confirmation! God had lined up all the details just in time, and Jerry was on his way. How big is your God!

4

The God Who Provides

Child Evangelism Fellowship Saskatchewan

Fall 1968–Summer 1973

What did he get himself into? There were so many things to learn, and so much to do in directing the work for CEF in western Saskatchewan. The land area was huge—everything west of Moose Jaw and Saskatoon, and everything from the North West Territories to the US border.

The main job description was to set up Good News Clubs® in the winter months, and 5-Day Clubs in the summer. That included looking for club hosts, recruiting and training the teachers, raising the finances, putting out newsletters, and working with the local committee to properly administer the work. He boarded with the family of one of the committee members in Swift Current, and set to work. Thankfully, a good foundation had already been laid by Dorothy Rempel (now Smith) who was leaving for Costa Rica with CEF.

Jerry was really touched by the people who told him they would join his financial support team including some former Sunday School teachers, employers, and Bible School professors. How amazing that they would send monthly support for his ministry when there were so many other young people who had gone into worthwhile ministries and needed support as well.

Somehow, through all the responsibilities of his new role, he still managed to nurture his relationship with me. During that winter, I worked in Calgary for the Royal Insurance Company calculating auto insurance renewal premiums. Jerry knew if he didn't write, he wouldn't get a letter from me. I had been raised in an era where a girl chasing after a guy was not considered proper. Occasionally, there were even short phone calls. Long-distance communications are so much easier now with email and all the text messaging devices. We both looked forward to Christmas time, 1968, when I was to travel with Jerry and another couple down to Wausau, Wisconsin to celebrate the holidays with his family. We had been dating for about 2 ½ years by that time. Jerry went to the Wausau Immanuel Baptist Church office one day and finally took the plunge to call my dad for permission to marry me.

Who knows the images that flashed through Dad's mind that day? Perhaps Dad thought about what had precipitated Jerry's very first date with me. Apparently, or so the story goes, some of the guys in the dorm were playing a game of Rook, and the loser's plight was to call up and ask out one of the principal's daughters! Jerry lost that day! Or perhaps Dad was reminded of the sound of Jerry's sports car that could be heard a block or two away with its Hollywood muffler. Or maybe he remembered one of the first times Jerry had been invited to our home for Sunday dinner. Dad suggested Jerry might be more comfortable taking off his sports jacket. Jerry declined at first, because he knew his secret would be discovered. You see, while attending college, the men were responsible for their own laundry, including ironing the 100% cotton dress shirts; but Jerry had devised a short cut. One simply needed to iron the collar and the front, as the rest was hidden underneath the suit jacket. Needless to say, when Dad encouraged Jerry again to slip off his jacket, we all enjoyed a good chuckle!

There was a pause on the phone as Dad considered his response to this bold young man who had had the courage to date the principal's daughter. And then Dad said, "I guess so." When Jerry asked what he meant by that, Dad said he had been guessing so for a long time! It was December 30th, on top of Rib Mountain in Wausau, when Jerry officially asked the question and we got engaged. Mom Robinson was excited when we got back to their house to share our news, but Dad Robinson only managed a "That's nice," before rolling over and going back to sleep.

With a big Swift Current, Saskatchewan CEF banquet planned for March 10, and our wedding set for May 10, it was hard for Jerry to keep the dates sorted out. Somehow he got through both events on the right days, and after a short honeymoon in Banff, we set off together for the three-month CEF Training Institute in Michigan.

What a diverse mix of people made up our class. The first ones we encountered were an older couple from England trying to communicate with a young man from Alabama. As Canadians, we quickly sized up the difficulties and stepped in to interpret from English to English! The students were of all ages and from a variety of countries. As we attended classes together, it was a great learning experience just to hear their stories and catch their concern for lost boys and girls around the world.

We even got in some early morning tennis matches and late afternoon water volleyball games in the nearby lake. It was all good until Jerry's wedding band flipped off into the water and sunk. We saw the spot where it hit, but we searched and raked the sandy bottom in vain. It was gone. At least it had lasted for three weeks! And I am sure the jeweler remembered us longer than average when we went back with our sad tale to purchase a second ring.

When we got back to Swift Current that fall, we often felt overwhelmed by the ministry responsibilities, marriage adjustments, and bare-bone finances. We moved into a little furnished second-floor apartment that our committee men had located for us. It was rather interesting. There were no cupboards or counter in the kitchen and there was just a single sink in one corner. The furnishings also lacked a kitchen table. The bathroom was a huge room, complete with a large storage cupboard and an old-fashioned tub with fancy legs that stood on the floor. Of course the only plug-in for shaving was on the far wall across the room from the sink. Jerry had to use an extension cord. The living room was something else! It was so tight that, when we had an overnight guest, his head touched one wall, and his feet, the other. But it was home—for a month.

We made about $180 per month. CEF provided a car and a credit card for the gas, but even a $5 parking ticket was a challenge. Once, when we did not make it back to the car in time, we decided we might as well go finish our errands since we already had the ticket. However, when we returned to our car again, we found a second ticket!

I remember grumbling one morning about only having bologna to eat…again! We had bologna in sandwiches, we had it in a casserole with scalloped potatoes, we fried it, and we had it cold. We did have one frozen chicken but I was saving that for when Jerry's folks came to visit. Jerry was sympathetic with my growing aversion to bologna, but he suggested we pray about it instead of complaining. So we did.

Shortly after we prayed, the phone rang; and some people we had never met invited us over for supper. They told us they had been storing some CEF material since the previous CEF director had left. They were wondering if we might like to see what was there, and take it home. That night, we enjoyed a wonderful meal. When the man heard we were moving into an unfurnished basement suite at the end of the month, he offered to make us a desk out of scrap lumber. It would have two filing drawers on each side which could be set on top of one another or could be used as a desk with a removable desktop. What a blessing! We still use that desk.

As we were heading out the door to go home, the lady said, "Just a minute." She had her husband run downstairs and bring up two shopping bags full of frozen meat including several roasts and packages of sirloin steaks. They had just butchered a cow. When we got in the car, we cried. How does bologna turn into sirloin steaks? God does it!

After a month in the makeshift upstairs apartment, we moved into a wonderful two-bedroom basement suite for $100 per month. What a blessing Mrs. Agnes Ponich, our landlady, was to us! It was almost like having a second mom. Lots of times she would have supper ready for us when we got home, and often our laundry was all done. A cook at the hospital, she was a capable teacher to show me how to make bread, buns, piecrusts, and Mennonite dishes like wareneki or perogies and roll kuchen.

And God continued to provide. Once we were given ten pounds of frozen corn and ten pounds of shelled frozen peas. Another time the doorbell rang upstairs. Although Jerry was up helping our landlady with a project, the man got directed to our back door entrance. When I answered, the man handed me 15 dozen eggs. One of his regular customers was away, so he brought the eggs to us. I didn't ask his name, thinking Jerry would have met him upstairs. And Jerry didn't find out his name, thinking the man would introduce himself to me downstairs. To this day, we have no idea where the eggs came from.

One spring, we were planning to make a weeklong trip north to visit clubs in our area and end up in Saskatoon for a CEF banquet. Our support cheque had not yet arrived before it was time to leave. We had $2.51 in our wallets and the credit card from CEF for the gas. In Saskatchewan, we didn't worry about places to stay or meals on the road as the rural people were very hospitable. In fact, we usually had to turn down invitations. However, when we got to Saskatoon and were on our way in to the banquet, we discovered that the tickets were not free. We never charged for our Swift Current banquets. We were a little embarrassed as we didn't have the cash and wondered what we were going to do. While standing in line, the man behind us began visiting with us. He was on the CEF committee for the Saskatoon area. Soon we reached the front of the line, and just then, the man behind leaned past us and said, "Oh, I am buying your tickets for you tonight." Thank you, Lord! By the time we got back home from that trip, we had $10.24, two chickens, a cabbage head and some canned goods. How big is your God?

Another time we had been encouraged to order a front quarter of beef. We were not quite sure how we were going to pay for it, but it would not be ready for several days. Just before the meat was due, Jerry's folks came through on their way back from Calgary to Wisconsin. His Mom had cashed in the coupons on a Canada Savings Bond she had purchased for Jerry when he was a kid. The amount came to $46, and our meat bill was $47. What great timing!

After all my music background, I really missed having a piano after we got married. We did not even have a record player. Some families had inquired about me teaching piano lessons to their children, so we began saving, and saving, and saving! After checking out options for where and what to buy, we thought we were getting close to our target amount—almost a thousand dollars. That was before we went to a special missionary meeting and both felt challenged to give the piano savings fund away. Just a couple days later, we received a letter from Jerry's grandparents. They had decided to give each of their grandchildren an early inheritance gift of $1,000. We were overwhelmed. It was as if a little voice was reminding us, "How big is your God? Is He big enough?" Shortly after, we bought our Yamaha piano—new for $932—and were so grateful to God for His provision.

The stories of God's supply have been an ongoing saga over the years. Our girls used to stand in front of me while I did their hair with the curling iron. They would point to something I was wearing and say, "Where did this come from? And where did this come from?" all the way down my apparel. Or they would look around our house and see our various furniture items. Each one was another story of God's provision. What a blessing for our children to witness God's care in so many unexpected ways.

It was a stretch for us, just starting out in ministry, to teach the Bible college students out at Pambrun, Saskatchewan who had signed up to teach Good News Clubs. I was still just 20 years of age, although I had graduated from Berean and worked for a year before getting married. But every other week, our task was to hold training classes for the students on how to weave the gospel message into their lessons, how to teach music and memory verses to boys and girls, and how to counsel children for salvation, assurance and Christian growth. We also visited their clubs, evaluating and encouraging them. We put in very long hours, preparing lessons, workshops, visuals, promotional items, and so much more. Often we felt very inadequate for the tasks. But God blessed the work, and the outreach to the boys and girls expanded. We ran about 30 Good News Clubs during the winter months and 115 outdoor 5-Day Clubs in 105 towns in the summer.

I remember lining up clubs in Gravelbourg, SK. It was a predominantly Catholic town, and when we tried to make arrangements, it was obvious that the people were not comfortable taking part in any program that was not sanctioned by the local priest. Jerry found out where he lived and went to pay him a visit. He explained that we were trying to arrange for a backyard club in the town. The priest questioned him about what they did at the club. Jerry told him about the singing, contests, continued missionary story and Bible stories that would be a part of each club meeting. The priest asked, "How long did you say it runs?"

Jerry said, "Just one hour each day for five days."

"Oh," smiled the priest, "I'm sure it's okay for the kids to go. After all, what can happen in one hour a day for one week?" Well, how big is your God?

One summer, we had the privilege of personally conducting a 5-Day Club in a little town a few miles east of Swift Current. Driving home from club Monday morning, we were just approaching Waldeck when we sensed God's urging to see about having a club there as well. In less than two hours, 36 eager faces were waiting for club to begin. On the Thursday, nine-year-old Randy invited Jesus to come into his heart. When asked how he knew Jesus really came in, he solemnly replied, "I feel the glory of God!" After we explained more, Randy left with his assurance based on God's Word, not just on his feelings. Our hearts were thrilled with 18 children who decided to become members of God's family during that impromptu week of 5-Day Club at Waldeck.

Part of our job was to provide our teachers with teaching resources. We put together material kits for $20 that included all the visualized songs and verses, Bible lessons, contests and extra stories. Then we looked for sponsors that would purchase the kits for the teachers and also become the prayer partners for a specific club. Even our landlady recruited several sponsors from her contacts at the hospital. Over several years, the teachers were able to acquire a good selection of excellent teaching materials that could be used again and again.

We also provided teacher training for our teachers. In the scattered, rural locations, we would try to visit their clubs once or twice during the winter season, and offer suggestions and helps. One club was held in a tiny town with the big name of Major, Saskatchewan—Mrs. G.'s club. Her club reports arrived very faithfully, averaging about 10 to 12 children each week. Her home was humble, but welcoming. After school, the children all trooped in and got ready for the club.

We were ready, too, with paper and pen in hand, to jot down evaluation notes for our after-club review. The first song announced was the "Stop Song," a familiar CEF visualized chorus. There was just one problem. We did not recognize the tune. And when we sang it through the second time, the song tune was different again! We began to get a little worried. Then it was Bible reading time. Everyone had his or her Bible, and Mrs. G. fumbled in the lesson manual to find the passage. It covered two or three chapters, and the class read every word. Next was lesson time. Mrs. G. got her flannel board ready, opened her manual, and began to read it, word for word. When the manual said, *"Place figure #3 on the board,"* Mrs. G. would sort through her flannel graph figures and smack figure #3 on the flannel scene. It was really irrelevant to her where the figure landed—or at least it seemed that way to us. By this time, we had put away our paper and pen, and were just silently praying for some graceful conclusion to this situation. But the amazing thing was that the children just sat there and took it all in.

When the club was at last over, and Mrs. G. was helping the children with coats and take-home verses, Jerry had occasion to chat with a 13-year-old girl. "How do you like this club?" Jerry asked.

"Oh, it is wonderful," she said. "Mrs. G. gives me her lesson stuff when she's done; and I teach it in the United Church down the block, just like Mrs. G. does. Mrs. G.'s daughter went to Prairie Bible School; and when I grow up, I want to go there, too. I want to be a teacher, just like Mrs. G.!"

When the children were all gone, Mrs. G. came to us and asked, "How did I do?"

We said, "You did just fine!" Mrs. G. could likely never have mastered all the teaching tips and skills that we offered; but God was still using her, just the same, to change the lives of boys and girls in that little town. Our God is a big God—perfectly able to use anyone yielded to Him.

Rallies and banquet times were big events in Swift Current. We rented the largest places we could find. One year, we had had a series of lessons on Moses during the winter Good News Clubs. At the rally that spring, we had lined up across the stage some of the homes (painted fridge boxes) in Egypt that were visited during the night of the Passover. In each home, when the door was opened, a banner was hanging that spelled "DEATH." Only one home that had blood sprinkled on the doorposts had the word "LIFE" on the banner inside. Another year, we used the theme of "Jesus is coming back again—but we don't know when." We made a giant joyntette astronaut figure on a pole that would raise his arms and legs when we pulled a cord. Whenever the kids saw the astronaut move, they were to jump to their feet and yell, "Maranatha." It was really something to see all those kids with their eyes glued to the astronaut! One year, we had the Gospel Messengers Quartet as special music for the rally, and 700 people came.

Teresa came to the rally too. She was twelve, and was one of the children in the home where Jerry first boarded in Swift Current. Afterwards, Teresa stayed behind for counseling. Jerry asked her why she was staying. She said she wanted to receive Christ as her Savior from sin. Jerry was puzzled. He knew she had always gone to Sunday School, and had been raised in a Christian home. Surely she would have had opportunities to receive Christ before as a young child. He asked her if she had ever prayed to receive Christ's gift of salvation before. "No," she said. "When I was little, everyone thought I was too little to invite Jesus into my life. Then, when I got older, I knew all the right answers; so everyone thought I already was a Christian." What a privilege it was, that day, to show the plan of salvation again to Teresa and give her the opportunity to respond to Christ before any more years went by.

For our annual free promotional banquets, we would ask the ladies from various churches to supply potato salads, jelly salads, and pies. One of the ladies on our committee would get up very early to make all the buns on banquet day for the 400 to 500 people that usually came. CEF would supply the meat— usually ham and Mennonite smoked farmer sausage. One year, Jerry went to pick up the meat from Dyck Packers. When he pulled out the credit card to pay, the cashier said, "We don't take credit cards today."

"Would you take a cheque?" Jerry asked.

"No, cheques won't work either."

Jerry was flustered. "But I don't have enough cash on me. I'll have to come back for the meat," he said.

By this time, the cashier was smiling. "The meat is free today!" Wow—meat for a whole banquet!

We usually brought in one speaker to speak at all three CEF banquets in the province. One year, the speaker was Pete Unrau, who had formerly been one of Dad Robinson's youth pastors. He got up and shared that once, when he was Jerry's youth pastor, he had backed Jerry up against the wall in a moment of frustration and said, "If God can change you, God can do anything." Now, years later, as Pete observed the ministry outreach Jerry was involved in, he told the audience, "God *can* do anything!"

Another speaker was Mel Johnson, a youth speaker from Minneapolis, Minnesota. He spoke at the Regina banquet first and then up north in Saskatoon, the two major cities in the province. On the way down to the Swift Current banquet, he was amazed at the lack of traffic. He said he only passed three cars in the 2 ½ hour drive. He knew that Swift Current was a much smaller city, but he could not believe his eyes when he arrived to find over 500 people at our Swift Current banquet. Where did they all come from? The people came from all the little towns and farms. This was a big event for Swift Current.

In spite of the thriving ministry, Jerry and I sensed it was time for a change by the spring of 1973. We were getting burned out with the work stresses. Since, at that time, there was no provincial director, we had to assume several extra responsibilities that were usually handled at the provincial level. While we were asked to consider taking on that role, we didn't feel like the provincial job, with even more administration, was the task God wanted for us. We had a growing desire to focus on doing children's meetings ourselves, not just mostly lining up children's ministry for others to do. It was timely that, at that point, God provided two capable young ladies who were willing to take over our work as area directors. With mixed emotions, we put in our resignation to CEF with the intention of doing more hands-on children's ministry.

5

Two Years with Lasting Results

Grace Church, Abbotsford

Fall 1973–Fall 1975

Our thoughts of doing Kids Krusades did not immediately materialize. At that time, CEF was not set up to accommodate a special ministries team for children's meetings and teachers' workshops. Its full-time staff members were administrating others, not focusing on teaching children directly. But we knew that we needed to work under *some* umbrella organization. However, God knew we needed some further preparation first.

After spending the summer of 1973 back in Calgary doing maintenance for Berean Bible College and waiting upon the Lord for the next step, we accepted an invitation to serve as the pastor's assistant at Grace Church in Abbotsford. The pastor there had gotten to know us while he was serving a church in

Swift Current, and he wanted us to come join his growing ministry out at the coast.

We were hit with many changes. There was the weather—much warmer, and much wetter! The first winter we almost ran out to take a picture of the sun when it did finally emerge from the rain clouds. Then there was the affluence. Young couples were starting off in homes much nicer than most Saskatchewan couples in their mid-fifties owned. And for the first time, we were looking from the inside out—how a local church views all the outside ministries that approach it for resources. In Swift Current, we tended to judge a church's spirituality by how it responded to CEF. God had some lessons to teach us.

When we arrived at Grace Church, the congregation was just moving into a lovely new facility. The pastor was working through and preaching on Campus Crusade materials, really emphasizing basic Christian principles, and teaching the people to share those principles with others—"Transferable Concepts." The church was growing. There was lots of work to do!

We worked mostly with the Christian Education Departments, finding department heads and volunteer staff for the Sunday School, the nursery, the library, and the youth. There was a core group of young people but they were not reaching out to fringe kids, and there was nothing much geared for junior highs or college age kids. We made the bold decision to divide the groups and find key adult sponsors to work with each. The kids were assigned into planning groups to work with the sponsors. Each month we would have a Bible study, a service-focused activity such as visiting shut-ins, and an outreach event.

One of our outreach events was a missing person's party at Stanley Park in Vancouver. Several people from our youth group were selected to disguise themselves as naturally as possible and wander through Stanley Park. The rest of the kids were to see how many of the "missing people" they could spot. There was Clara, dressed as a nurse pushing a patient in a wheel chair through the park. Today she is a field director with SIM in Africa. Tom sat in front of his easel, painting in the park. Tom, now a Calgary lawyer, has helped us on several occasions with ministry legal issues. Jerry was dressed as a little old granny. It was a great disguise, except when he had to use the washroom. Which one do you choose? And when Jerry had to change out of his disguise behind some bushes, he got into a predicament. He needed help to undo his "bra." Thankfully, Sharon was nearby. Sharon and her husband, Russ, have served for many years as a Pastor couple with the Mennonite Brethren conference in Manitoba. Jerry still cannot figure out how ladies maneuver to undo those undergarment hooks behind their backs!

As we recruited volunteers and mentored individuals, we had no idea how it was laying a foundation in people's lives. Besides setting up his own thriving business, Larry took on the challenge as Sunday School Superintendent and later served in many leadership roles at Grace Church and in the Conference for the Fellowship of Evangelical Bible Churches. Ken got started in the right direction through a home Bible Study and involvement with the youth. He and his wife, Helga, have been involved at Grace Church in various ways including music, sound operations, and the missions committee. Bob has quietly done house-to-house visitation for many years. Several others also went on to serve in key roles in their churches or headed overseas in missions. And little did we know that the friends and contacts we made during those two years in Abbotsford would become a solid base of financial and prayer support for the many years of our ministry to follow.

In spite of the church outreach potential, Jerry was only on half-time salary for the first year. He supplemented our income with various part-time jobs including custodial service for the public schools and some casual work for a local businessman. We were used to making do on a limited income. The hourly wage that the businessman was paying seemed excessive to us for what was being accomplished. His other employees were aghast when they heard that Jerry had spoken to the boss about over-payment. They all felt they were underpaid!

We rented housing during the time we were in Abbotsford. At first, the church had lined up a home for us to rent where the owners were on an extended trip to Africa to visit their missionary kids. Not too many people could brag about having an elevator in their home, but we could! They had transformed a closet into an elevator.

When those folks came home, we moved around the block into a home that was tied up in an estate settlement. It was a place that produced some great memories. We were even able to fit a small pool table into the basement. That was a great point of contact with youth from the church. And it gave me special delight to win against some of the guys! Even Happy, the Saint Bernard pup from next door, loved to come and watch the action outside the basement window. There was one problem. She would drool saliva all down the window, fog it up with her breath, and then would try to lick it clean again so she could see through it. She loved that yard—coming over and drinking great gulps from our hose when we watered the garden. We found massive paw prints in the flowerbeds and vegetable garden. That was okay with us. We were not very experienced gardeners at that point. For example, we bought vegetable seeds and tried to follow the instructions. The instructions on the plastic package of bean seeds were a bit confusing. They said, "Cut the bubble to dispense the seeds." Jerry insisted that we needed to slice each little seed exterior on the colored spot to let out the seed! I finally convinced him that it was just the packaging that the instructions were referring to. One summer, we planted way too many cucumbers. After eating, and canning, and giving away all we could, we had great fun having mushy yellow cucumber wars with the boys nearby. So many lessons to learn!

As our time in the second home was running out, we checked into the possibilities of purchasing a home. A man, connected to the church, was selling some townhouses that seemed manageable with the monthly payment we could afford. We were good savers and had no debt, but the mortgage people were not impressed with our salary figures. The seller had a quick solution. He said he would vouch for me that I was on his payroll, and then we would easily qualify. It was tempting, but there was one problem. It was not true. Did God need our deception to supply our needs? It was hard to turn down the possibility of home ownership at that point, but we both felt clean and at peace as we looked for another place to rent.

The church work was growing and vibrant during those years. Just before we came, there had been about 200 people attending. But with the move to the new building, and with the outreach efforts, the attendance grew to around 450 or more. We even had to take out some walls in the small Sunday School classrooms in order to accommodate the growing numbers. We held open houses, had a bus ministry, and ran special children's meetings—Kids Krusades. I remember about the fourth day of the children's meetings, Jerry was in the middle of telling his continued missionary story. As I scanned over the crowd of kids, I watched a dilemma unfold right before my eyes. A little boy was sitting in the front row, squirming and holding himself. His eyes were glued to the visual and on Jerry, telling the story. All of a sudden, he couldn't hold it any longer; and a little puddle began to emerge on the floor at his feet. At the end of the meeting, his mother arrived and scolded him. "Why didn't you go to the bathroom?" she asked.

"Well, Mom, I had a tough choice to make—go to the bathroom and miss the story, or stay to hear what happened. You can always go to the bathroom, but the story wouldn't wait!"

Holding those Kids Krusades at Grace Church was a reminder to us of what we had dreamed of doing when we first left CEF in Saskatchewan. It seemed the Lord kept bringing back that desire to minister directly to children.

Besides being drawn by that dream, we were also struggling with the dynamics of our position on the pastoral staff at the church. What really was a pastor's assistant? Was it just an extension of the pastor? Jerry couldn't be the pastor's clone. How did this job fit with our gifting? Was there any freedom to dream and develop areas of ministry in the way we could best do it? Those issues finally led Jerry to make another decision. It was time to resign again—this time to move back to Alberta where we had many more contacts, and to begin working into what we felt God had called us to do—hands-on children's ministry. Besides, we still had no family of our own, so we would be free to travel as necessary. Also, by this time, Child Evangelism Fellowship had enlarged its sphere to encompass a children's ministry team like we envisioned; so at last it seemed like we had a green light.

Almost! The businessman Jerry had worked for part-time offered us the use of one of his work trucks to move our belongings back to Calgary. He had a branch business there and needed to transport to Calgary a generator that was arriving from the States. He said the truck would be ready for us about the end of September. The day came and went, and the generator had not yet come in from the States. Each day we checked, and each day we waited.

After two weeks, and lots of prayer, one day I said to Jerry, "Maybe there is something the Lord wants us to do yet before we move. Let's go talk to Bill."

Bill was not a Christian, but came faithfully to church with his wife, Doreen. They had both opened their home to the College and Career group, and we had enjoyed getting to know Bill. He was quite a character with a real sense of humor that kept everyone laughing. He drove back and forth to North Vancouver to work, so he had to be up very early each day for the perilous commute.

We called and asked if they were free for us to come over and visit that evening. "Sure!" they said.

We chatted a bit and then got playing a game of Rook. All evening we played, until it was well past time for us to be leaving. Bill had to get to bed!

We said our goodbyes and headed to the car. But I was troubled. "Jerry," I said, "we came to talk to Bill about the Lord and we didn't do that at all!"

"You're right!" Jerry agreed. "What do we do now?"

We prayed. And then we went back to the front door and rang the bell.

"Robinson, what do you want now?" Bill grumbled as he opened the door.

"Bill, we came tonight to talk to you about the Lord, and we didn't do it."

"Well, you better come back in, then," he said.

For the next couple hours, we shared again with Bill the simple plan of salvation and tried to answer his questions. Then he said, "Well, we better get down on our knees and get this settled."

What a thrill to hear Bill invite Jesus Christ to be his Savior that night. And then, middle of the night or not, Bill and Doreen had to call her sister Marg and family to tell them the great news! Bill still calls Jerry his "Dad" (spiritual Dad) even though he is older than Jerry.

And the next morning—our truck was ready! How big is your God!

6

PURSUING A PASSION

Kids Krusades

Fall 1975–Fall 1979

It took a while to get established as a Special Ministries Team under CEF. There were children's presentations and training workshops to develop. Promotional items had to be created and printed. Churches had to be contacted about our availability to hold teachers' workshops and Kids Krusades. Meanwhile, Ambassador Baptist Church in Calgary, now Varsity Bible Church, invited us to work in the area of Christian education on an interim basis and to whatever extent we were able, while we began to move into the new ministry. We appreciated this opportunity to be involved in Christian education and, at the same time, be able to cover our expenses during the transition; but our time there was short-lived.

Before long, we found ourselves needing to devote "full-time" to the new ministry as we were spending about three weeks of every four on the road doing children's ministry and teachers' workshops. Most summers and a number of winter weekends were spent speaking at camps, but we also filled many invitations from communities in western Canada and some locations in the States to hold week-long series of children's meetings.

On the rare occasions that we traveled with Jerry's folks, Rev. George & Inez Robinson, we seldom got far before Dad Robinson was pointing out the window saying, "I had special meetings in that community," or, "I preached in that church over there," or, "I met so-and-so in that town when they invited me to speak at their conference." Now our own children experience the same conversations from us. We held Kids Krusades in Hanna, Calgary, Abbotsford, 100 Mile House, Penticton, Port Alberni, Port Coquitlam, Vancouver, Cloverdale, Hythe, Edmonton, Fort St John, Burns Lake, Fraser Lake, Coronation, Salmon Arm, Warman, Red Deer, Silver Creek, Irma, Viking, Leslieville, Whitecourt, Crossfield, , Estevan, Coronach, Camrose, Grand Centre, and Bonnyville in western Canada, as well as in Jamestown ND, and Wausau WI. We went back to some of these communities a second and third time; and in some of the larger centers, we held meetings in more than one location.

Even though our presentations were not high tech and flashy, we did our best to attractively and faithfully share the gospel each day, as well as challenge Christian children to grow in their relationship with God. And the children came! I wish you could have seen no less than forty kids pile out of a van that was picking up children from a little town just out of Estevan, Saskatchewan. That was before seat belt legislation. In fact, that event probably prompted it! That same week we had so many older kids enthused about the special meetings that we had to open a new contest category for the junior high age group.

Each community we visited had its own unique atmosphere. But they all had children: tall ones, short ones, smart ones, mischievous ones, attractive ones, and ones that were not so attractive. Some came from solid Christian homes, some did not know who their parents were, some were athletic, some could not carry a tune, some were show-offs, and some would not talk at all. But we knew that when God looked at them, He saw two kinds of children—those who had received Christ as their Savior from sin, and those who had not. What a responsibility to share the gospel with so many boys and girls. What a privilege!

So often we realized we were on the battlefront. Satan bids high for the lives of boys and girls. In some towns we could really sense the oppression. During a week in one of those dark communities, we felt particularly under spiritual attack. We did have a number of children pray to receive Christ that week, but at night I would battle with powerful doubts: *"How do you know that what you are teaching those kids is really true? How do you know for sure there is a God? What makes you think a child can savingly believe? Do you really think what you are doing will make a difference in these kids' lives? Why waste your time doing this?"*

When we left that town, we headed down the Fraser Canyon to the lower mainland of BC. In many places the road hugged the Fraser River with sharp drop-offs to the right. Jerry usually did most the driving, but sometimes I would spell him off. I happened to be driving that leg of the highway when I was suddenly overwhelmed with a powerful urge to drive right off the road into the Fraser River and experience the sensation of our car being flooded with water. The presence of evil was almost stifling. I woke Jerry and asked him to pray for God's protection over us through the precious blood of the Lord Jesus Christ. There is a reason why God gives us the spiritual armor of protection in Ephesians 6. We do have a powerful enemy. *"But greater is He that is in you, than he that is in the world"* (1 John 4:4). After praying, we continued safely on our way to the next Kids Krusade location.

Another spiritual attack happened in Red Deer on the first evening of the week of children's meetings. The church was packed, but the atmosphere was hard. There were boys in the back row that were disruptive. Jerry always told the children in our meetings that we had just one rule: "Only one person talks at once." He would go on to explain: "If I'm talking, that means you need to be quiet. If you want to do all the talking, I'll sit down and we'll listen to you. But then you'll miss all the stories and contests and prizes and things. Everyone gets one chance. After that I'll ask you to leave." We tried to be consistent with that, and usually enjoyed controlled audiences. But that evening there was just a festering buzz, and it was hard to catch any one person talking. Finally, Jerry spoke to one of the troublemakers and sent him home with the reminder he was welcome to come back the next night if he was willing to listen. Afterwards, we called some people in that church and asked them to pray for the atmosphere. The next evening was as different as night and day. What had changed? Only God had turned it around.

Needless to say, living in different people's homes week after week was both a blessing and a challenge. We met many wonderful people. And we knew it was a real sacrifice on their part to open their homes to us for a whole week. There were some locations that really stood out in our memories. One was staying for the week in a bedroom that was right above a funeral home. Our imaginations had to be reined in a few times that week.

Another week we were billeted with a wonderful French Canadian family living on Vancouver Island. They were new Christians and treated us with great honor—likely as you might expect to treat a Priest. Our meetings were held early in the evening; so when we arrived home, the lady would fuss over us with something to drink, articles to read, seating us by the fire place with a foot stool pulled up under our feet, and so on. During the last meal with them, we ate by candlelight; and she played us a recording of their entire wedding ceremony—in French! One evening was especially memorable. That night, our hostess outdid herself, trying to serve us. She kept insisting that we go put on our pajamas and get comfortable to sit by the fireplace in the living room. I was just as insistent that I was comfortable as I was. But Jerry...well...he can rarely say "No" to anybody. Trying to think of a good excuse, he said, "I don't have a housecoat with me."

"Oh," she said, "I'm sure my son's housecoat would fit you." And off she ran to get it. Her son was 12 years old! She came back with the housecoat and pulled Jerry up, steering him down the hall towards the bedroom. I wondered what in the world he would find to serve as pajamas. Ever since he had a dream as a child that he was gagging on marshmallows and woke up to find his pajama buttons missing, he has not supported the pajama industry.

He was gone a long time. He told me later, that he was in full-blown panic. His eyes lit on the white long-johns his Grandpa Shatto had passed on to him when we visited his grandparents en route through Kelowna. Since his grandpa was not using the long-johns much in the milder Kelowna climate, he figured Jerry might as well take them. How could he have known how soon those long-johns would come in handy? When Jerry finally emerged in his "comfortable" lounging gear, I almost doubled over laughing. He was quite a sight, looking like a pixie with white tights and a too-short housecoat over top. The hostess didn't make any comment, but at least she did not press him to "get comfortable" again that week!

Then there was the pastor's home in one community. We were to hold meetings in two neighboring towns that week. When it was time to retire the first night, the pastor's wife, who worked in the local hospital, took us downstairs to show us the room. She apologized that they had little puppies down there that might want to visit us. The moment she opened the basement door, the aroma hit us. The mother and pups were using the basement as their open range outhouse. It was powerful! The pastor's wife directed us to the makeshift bedroom, and pointed at a little basement washroom across the open area.

After she headed back upstairs, we began to assess how we would manage for the week. The bathroom was filthy. We found a bleach bottle by the laundry area, and tried to do some basic cleaning—toilet seat and shower floor—so we could use the necessities without embarrassing our host with a major overhaul. When we opened the bed, we discovered stained flannel sheets with residual hair. After crawling into bed the first night, we guessed where the stains and hair came from. The bed had broken springs that attacked you every time you moved. Likely the last victim that stayed there had suffered open wounds, or lost some body hair while trying to escape! Each night we would wait till the last possible hour before taking one final gulp of fresh air and then descending down to our quarters. One night, in the middle of the night, Jerry needed to get up and make the trek over to the little washroom. He had barely stepped past the bedroom door when I heard a muffled gasp. Sure enough, he had slipped in a fresh batch of dog poop on the floor. It was disgusting! But something hit me about the whole situation that put it all in a different light. If Christ, the King of Glory, was willing to leave all the wonders of heaven and endure the human birthing process in a smelly stable to come to rescue a lost world, who was I to think my sleeping accommodations that week were beneath me! Ours was such a minor sacrifice! It was a profound thought that really helped us through that week. We were glad, though, that we did not have to experience our hostess's care at the hospital!

We also discovered some other challenges with staying in people's homes during weeks of meetings. A schedule of study and preparation was difficult to maintain. One week we would be staying with farmers who were up at 6:00 a.m. The next week we might be billeted with a retired couple that wanted to sleep in till 9:00 a.m. Suppers were especially challenging as they often conflicted with us getting to the crusade ahead of time.

Another challenge had to do with my temperament. Jerry is a "people person," and when he is around people, he comes to life. For him, life on the road and getting to know people in their homes was totally stimulating. For me, on the other hand, being with people for extended periods was very draining. While I am comfortable speaking to an audience, even large groups, chatting in church foyers is something else. How do you wrap up an awkward conversation when you've run out of things to say, and gracefully move on to the next person? Usually, after we handled any counseling with boys and girls following the meetings, I would go pick up our visuals and things, getting them all in order for the next night, while Jerry would enjoy mingling with the people. But then we'd go back to our host family of the week and visit some more.

The crunch came when I started breaking out in hives every weekend as we moved to another community. Even though I thought I was coping with managing all the changes and new expectations of each setting, my system was telling me otherwise. My hives would just clear up, and then it was time to move on again to a new situation. More hives!

We were so grateful when God provided us with a new 19' travel trailer to take along. Now I could have some down time away from people each day. We could still be billeted out for lunches, but we could eat light suppers in the trailer on our own timeframe so we could be ready for the meetings early. What a difference that made! Of course the trailer accommodation was not suitable for winter months, but for the rest of the year it was home.

It was during summer ministry at camp in 1978 that I began to feel very tired. I had been sick with a heavy cold; but even when the cold was gone, I was still dragging. I wondered if I was just played out from the heavy ministry responsibilities, and my body was craving sleep. Jerry finally suggested I make an appointment with the doctor.

When I got back to the camp after my appointment, I told Jerry he had better sit down. I really did have a disease. Jerry's immediate thought was that I had cancer. "But," I added, "in nine months I will be okay." After almost ten years with no children, neither of us expected this turn of events. We could hardly believe I was pregnant! Even when our son, Jeremy, arrived March 18, 1979, I kept waiting for his parents to come and pick him up. But we were the parents! Amazing!

While it required a little more packing—baby and diaper bag—we continued with children's ministry, tackling an even heavier load of meetings than the previous year. By the fall of 1979, however, Jeremy was making strange. I can still remember hearing his screams at the back of Rockyview Alliance Church in Calgary. In fact, every night he screamed at his babysitter for the whole session of Kids Krusade. I began having doubts about inflicting more unsuspecting volunteer baby sitters in other settings. Maybe Kids Krusades were not for kids after all. Not mine anyway! Not at this stage! It was a difficult decision, but we felt it was time to curtail our "on-the-road" lifestyle in children's ministry and do what we could to reach children from one location. With that in mind, Jerry accepted the offer of a full-time position as director of Camp Chestermere.

7

REACHING KIDS, IMPACTING STAFF

Camp Chestermere

January 1, 1980–September 30, 1983

How Jerry ever ended up as a camp director, I will never know. The only camp he remembers attending as a child, he didn't even finish out the week. The camp director sent him home!

But for me, growing up, camp had been a way of life. Since my dad had been the camp director at Chestermere back then, it was an automatic yearly event—first as a camper, and then as a counselor. I loved it. I spent the first half of each year looking forward to camp, and the last half looking back at the great summer memories.

As a couple, Jerry and I had been involved in various aspects of camp ministry even before taking on the director position at Camp Chestermere. First, we had served as the sports directors at a camp in Saskatchewan during our years in CEF there. It was a young teens' camp, and most of the kids were from farm communities. We divided them into teams for daily competitions. One afternoon, each team had to catch a live chicken, butcher it, pluck off the feathers, clean it, and cut it up for that evening's banquet. We let the cooks be the judges. I am afraid that some of the necks had more than one axe mark!

Then we had been camp speakers for several years, both for summer and winter weekend camps. We had seen how effective camp ministry was in the lives of many of the boys and girls who came. They saw Christianity at work in every facet of life for a whole week. We had also seen the importance of a strong counseling team, and what happens when the counselors were not held accountable and were not committed to God in their own lives. A speaker's job becomes almost impossible when the camp dynamics are not positively controlled. We figured if we were in charge of directing the camp, we could at least try to control some of those issues. But to actually step into the demanding responsibility of camp directing was a big, new challenge.

The first hurdle we faced at Camp Chestermere was getting the board to approve taking on Project 25 designed to raise $25,000 for the camp's 25th anniversary year. After God set things in motion with that timely phone call from the oilman during the camp board meeting (Chapter 1), it was a thrill to see God provide the additional funds. The projects included a new kitchen stove, a 12-passenger van, office equipment, dock improvements, a commercial dishwasher, and the completion and furnishing of a staff fireside room and lounge in the lodge basement.

Because of the necessity of having well-trained staff, we designed a two-week staff training camp. Besides becoming familiar with their assigned craft—canoeing, kayaking, archery, rowing, water-skiing, riflery, sailing, trampolining, or horsemanship—counselors learned and practiced how to weave the gospel message into the Bible lessons for their campers. They practiced how to counsel children for salvation or assurance. They learned how to effectively teach memory verses, and how the camp contest for that year would work. They prepared the morning and evening devotions they would share with their campers. It was a heavy couple of weeks, but it proved to be a highlight. And in the process, the summer staff forged friendships that would last a lifetime. Instead of scaring off potential counselors, the expectations seemed to attract them; and we even had to turn some away.

Our camp names were Sky Pilot and Co-Pilot since we tried to show boys and girls the way to heaven. Later, the camp board requested Jerry to officially become ordained in order to add credibility to his role as the camp's spiritual leader. It was especially helpful when he made contacts with campers' parents and aid organizations.

Every year we developed a new summer series. Each day told another segment of the theme. One year it was "Mission Impossible." Another year was "This is Your Story." We talked about how, even without being aware of it, we are all writing the story of our lives. We used contest cards designed like Monopoly Boards on which campers could collect signatures of their counselors as they bought up the opportunities that week: learning the daily verse, cleaning their cabin, learning extra verses, and so on. One summer we did a "Time Tunnel" theme. Each camper had to have a passport contest card for the week. A friend had created a time tunnel machine out of a fridge box. To prerecorded sound effects, Jerry would check the security features, test the communications systems, and push the activator switch, to send us back in time. He would then go into the box while the music finished playing; and I would emerge, back thousands and thousands of years to a Bible setting.

Every evening at campfire, we had a continued missionary story. A big screen had been erected—two 4′ x 8′ sheets of plywood side by side, painted white, and with a little topper to protect it from rain. The stories were visualized on colored transparencies. After the usual skits and fun songs, we would sing some gospel choruses, and then get into the story time, weaving the plan of salvation throughout. Each night, we left the story at a high point. And each night, we would give an invitation for campers to stay behind and talk about what it meant to receive Christ as Savior, or head off to their cabins for evening snack. It was amazing how many chose to stay and make sure of their relationship with Christ.

After the first camping season we got comments like these:

- "This week of Teen's Camp has been the best week of my summer."Marshall (15)
- "I've gone to church all my life but I've never heard the things you teach here. It makes a lot of sense."Cindy (16)
- "Thank you so much for all you've taught me about God and His way. I know it is right."Carmen (12)

I guess it was to be expected that Satan would try to foil what God wanted to do. Every summer, no matter how well prepared we tried to be, there were last-minute catastrophes. One year, the sewer backed up just before camp; and major repairs had to be done. How do you run a camp with no washroom facilities? Designating one side of the hedge a pink side and the other a blue side with toilet tissue on top was one suggestion—but we didn't take it. Just in time, the repair was made.

Another year, after orientating our summer program director for two months, we heard our doorbell ring. There stood the program director with our box of files. He was quitting. We were shocked. But God provided a replacement at the last minute. The same thing happened a different summer with our coordinator for the counselors-in-training.

Then there was the summer, right in the middle of camping season, when we got a knock on our trailer door, very early in the morning. My pastor, Bill Laing, was there to tell us that my dad had passed away during the night. I vaguely thought he must have been talking about my uncle who was expected to die any day after a long battle with cancer. But Dad? I could scarcely get it through my brain. Dad had died suddenly during the night from a ruptured aortic aneurysm. Now he would never get to meet our little Jennifer. We had just told him a couple weeks earlier that we were expecting our second child. Gone? Dad? It just didn't seem possible!

As Pastor Laing drove two-year-old Jeremy and me back into Calgary to be with my mom, Dad's favorite chorus kept running through my mind:

How Big Is Your God?

I'm going higher, yes higher someday,
I'm going higher someday,
Over the mountains, beyond the blue sky,
Going where none ever sicken or die
Into the land of the sweet by and by
I'm going higher someday.

What a comfort to know Dad was there! And what strength God gave as I shared the Bible lessons during chapels that next week of camp.

Each summer, five children's camps were offered. Then there was teens' camp and a 10-day wilderness camp. For young people age 14 and up, a two-year counselor-in-training program was offered and then further training extended through junior counselor status. Winter camps and reunions offered great follow-up opportunities with campers. When the camp was available, rental groups used the facilities. Each winter we catered to a number of banquets during the Christmas season, and Jerry actually got quite proficient at cooking turkeys. I really appreciated his advice when it was my turn to take over hosting our own family turkey dinners! Then early in January, Jerry was off to visit a number of colleges, seeking to recruit staff for the coming year. There were brochures and camp folders to design and print. And then there was the new summer series to develop. The workload was relentless, but the ministry potential was tremendous.

Once, after counseling two boys, one of them prayed, "Dear God, please forgive my sins. I want you to take them and throw them out the window and forget I ever did them." The other boy prayed, "O God, my sins are too bad, and I don't want you to throw them out the window, because someone might be going by and catch them, and I don't want anybody to catch my sins..."

Lisa was a camper who learned over seventy-five extra verses, and was voted the outstanding camper of the week. She told us that camp was a real spiritual highlight for her each year; and when we caught a glimpse of her home situation on closing night, we could understand why.

Another time, three girls came running up on the first day of camp saying, "We've been *spiritual breathing* ever since winter camp—not that we're perfect, but we keep putting God back on the throne." *Spiritual breathing* was a term we used to explain confession of sin (exhaling) and then putting Christ back on the throne of our lives (inhaling).

Eli was a 10-year old terror. He was disruptive, and perverted. We could not trust him with the other boys at winter camp—he kept trying to get into their sleeping bags—so we had him sleep in the lodge with only the dog for company. But what a change! Eli prayed to receive Christ that camp, and next summer Eli won the outstanding camper award.

Staff members were changed as well. Jerry first met Dan and his older siblings in Swift Current, Saskatchewan. His dad had served on our CEF committee, and his mom had hosted a Good News Club. Dan was full of life. One day, when we were there visiting, somehow Jerry got into a water fight with the kids outside. Dan got the bright idea to chase Jerry with the hose. Jerry headed into the house in a hurry. Dan followed. And that was when Dan's mother came to life! She was not impressed! We had a good laugh with her about the incident on a recent visit in her home, now in northern Alberta.

As Dan got older, he saw inconsistencies around him and he got into the wrong crowd. He was not doing well, into drugs and other things. We were on our way from Alberta to Regina, and stopped in for a brief visit with Dan's parents. His Mom shared her concern for Dan, and after supper, Jerry stopped by Dan's room. Jerry challenged him, "If you keep going the direction you are going, where will you be five years from now or ten years from now?"

Then Dan came to Camp Chestermere as a Junior Counselor. It was a risk. And there were some interesting situations—like the time Dan told one of his notorious campers, "Eddy, this is what I'd like to do to your head." With that, Dan smashed his fist against the cabin door, only to discover the door was solid wood. Dan's hand was in a cast for some weeks following. But something was happening. God was using the atmosphere and the truths at camp to have an impact. It was life changing. After a couple summers at camp, Dan went off to Bible school, and then became an Alliance pastor. In 2003, we got a letter from Dan. Part of it read:

> I can remember walking with (your son) Jeremy
> at Chestermere and listening as he told me of his
> invisible camels. Donna and I both turn 40 this
> year although I think there has got to be some
> mistake along the way since neither of us acts 40.
> We are celebrating our 9th year (pastoring at our
> church)…but somehow I have less to say this
> year. About a year ago I told Donna that I was

done, I had nothing left to say. In her wisdom, she reminded me that 'Maybe God has something to say.' It became the turning point in my preaching…I truly love being a pastor and can't imagine doing anything else…You have played such a vital role in my life, and in part, I owe who I am and what I do to your love and wisdom. I'm not certain if you have doubts about what you have done but I want you to know how much you transformed my life and I will always owe you a debt I cannot repay.

How humbling. How encouraging that God would take ordinary, imperfect people like us and use us to do His work in other lives.

And there was Tony, an older boy attending camp for the first time. After the first campfire, Tony stayed behind for counseling. Jerry shared what it meant to become a Christian, and how he could receive Christ. But tears filled his eyes, and he said he would think about it. He was not ready.

Each day we prayed for Tony, and each day he looked back longingly as he left chapel and campfire. Near the end of camp, Tony stayed again for a talk. "How are things going?" Jerry asked.

"Terrible!" said Tony. "I want to, and yet I don't." You could just see the battle going on inside Tony. This time they talked for over an hour, and Jerry explained how we need to settle it now because we have no guarantee of tomorrow.

"Tony," Jerry asked again, "do you want to receive Christ tonight?"

You could see the choice was being made as Tony's face got hard and he said, "No, I've got too much to give up." At the end of the last day of chapel, Jerry stood by the door. He looked over at Tony and their eyes met, but Tony didn't stay.

It was many years later, and we were browsing in a mall. The "SALE" sign caught Jerry's eye, so without looking at anything else, Jerry wandered into "Mr. Big and Tall." He was obviously in the wrong store. I have to shorten all his pants and the sleeves on his long-sleeve shirts! A store attendant turned to greet him, and there was Tony!

"Sky Pilot!" Tony exclaimed.

"Tony!" Jerry said. Do you remember where you were the last time I saw you? You were heading out of chapel. How are you doing?"

Tony brought Jerry up to date. He was living with his girl-friend and they were expecting a little baby.

"Tony, do you remember what you learned at camp?" Jerry asked. Tony nodded.

"Tony, you need to take your girlfriend and that little baby to church. Promise me you'll go to church this Sunday." And Tony nodded.

Who knows how Tony is doing today. Obviously, God was still pursuing Tony; and obviously, God had wanted Tony to be reminded again about the truths he had heard at camp. After all, it was not every day Jerry shopped at "Mr. Big and Tall."

So many kids came through camp. So many life stories were written. As much as we wanted everyone to choose God's way in his or her life, our responsibility was just to be faithful.

One day, as Jerry was sitting in his camp office, a taxi drove up. Jerry went out to offer his assistance. The lady that emerged said, "No thank you. You don't need to show me around. I know my way around here. I used to come to this camp as a child. I just want to walk around and feel God. God was in this camp." So, while the taxi waited for the better part of an hour, the lady relived her memories of bygone days at camp. Who can measure the impact God can have at camp!

8

Launching a Second Camp

Camp Little Red

First season, 1982

What was the best use of that special $30,000 gift from the oilman? It was still set aside. Meanwhile, the community around Camp Chestermere was growing. When I had been a camper, there were no homes on the west side of the lake, and the east shore had just small summer cottages. But in the early 1980s, beautiful permanent homes were being built around Chestermere Lake. Some were raising concerns about the future viability of the camp in that location as the area continued to become urbanized. The board prayed much about the long-term direction. Perhaps it was time to establish another camp property further out from the city limits to serve as backup in case relocation became necessary. We decided to investigate some property in central Alberta.

My dad had been a big part of initiating and purchasing the camp at Chestermere years earlier, when that property belonged to a Sea Cadet Camp. After serving for many years as the director and camp manager, Dad gradually turned over the leadership to others. Now, some 27 years later, the birthing and pioneering of a second camp location was underway. After much prayer, deliberation, and searching, another land purchase was made in the fall of 1981 for140 acres of land west of Bowden. What dreams we had for future ministry there! We gathered on October 4, 1981 with about 80 friends for the official dedication of the property that was to become Camp Little Red. My mom, Ethelwyn Cornell, was chosen by the board to turn the sod. Dad had passed away just three months previously, but I am sure he would have been delighted that day. A new camp was being launched.

The very first camping season at Camp Little Red happened the summer of 1982. There was so much to do to get the bare facility arrangements in place. The task seemed impossible, especially while still running all the programs at Camp Chestermere as well. But we have a God of the impossible.

There was the miracle of a crew from Black Diamond coming up for a rainy long weekend to build a corral, the miracle of getting lumber and gates from the Calgary stock yards at a fraction of the normal price, the miracle of Dome Petroleum moving in the cookhouse and building a road to it. And that was just the start. Then there was the miracle of a generator being provided, the miracle of farmers from Innisfail who came down early one day to load up all the horses from Chestermere and take them out to Camp Little Red, and the miracle of having men complete the fencing at Little Red the same day the horses arrived. There was even the miracle of the Seventh Day Adventist Camp nearby allowing us to use their water supply when our own arrangements fell through the day of camp opening. It seemed that the more challenges that arose, the more miracles God provided.

Then there were the actual weeks of camp—two of them—with 40 campers in each. And in spite of one camp having rain four out of five days, our campers were very enthusiastic about Camp Little Red and the potential there. During that first summer, 17 campers were counseled for salvation and another 30 for assurance, rededication, and other needs. What a faithful God we serve.

On February 18, 1983, after that first camping season, we held a banquet in Red Deer for the central Alberta area churches. It was potluck style with families bringing the food. One hundred and twenty-five came that night, including the children and the young people we'd asked to help serve. Jerry shared some of the stories of how the camp had started, from the oilman's gift, to the miracles of God's provision the previous summer.

After cleaning up, we drove back to Calgary. It was about 1:00 a.m. when the phone rang. The treasurer was on the line. "How much do you think came in for the camp tonight?" he asked.

Jerry knew what the offerings generally totaled at the Calgary banquets for Camp Chestermere. In fact, that year $3,300 had been given at the Chestermere banquet. With the smaller attendance in Red Deer, Jerry thought an offering of $3,000 would be wonderful.

"No, think bigger," said the treasurer.

"Maybe $5,000," said Jerry.

"Bigger," encouraged the man.

"Uhhhh, $10,000," said Jerry, feeling like he was going way out on a limb with such a figure.

"Are you sitting down?" asked the treasurer. "Just over $33,000 came in tonight!"

How big is your God? Wow! Again we were amazed and overwhelmed at what God had done.

Over the years it has been wonderful to see how the ministry and outreach of Camp Little Red has grown. Our own children attended as campers; and several of them went on to spend many summers serving as kitchen help, counselors, program directors, life-guards, camp nurse, and speakers. Recently, our daughter Jaclyn was orienting a first-time volunteer nurse at Camp Little Red. When Jaclyn asked her if she had ever been to camp before, she shared that she and two siblings, from an unchurched background, went to Camp Chestermere years ago and became Christians with Sky Pilot and Co-Pilot. The lady shared that her brother is now a pastor. All three are following the Lord! And now she was getting involved at Camp Little Red. Jaclyn told her, "Sky Pilot and Co-Pilot are my parents!" What a privilege God gave us to be part of camp ministry.

With the launching of the second camp, and still keeping up with all the responsibilities at Chestermere, it was no wonder Jerry was physically exhausted. By this time, the staff at Chestermere had expanded to include two other couples: a full-time program director and office manager, and a full-time cook and maintenance man. In spite of the extra help, we were wearing thin. We would just get one group of kids played out, and a fresh bunch would arrive the next week. Even though we tried to ensure that counselors and staff got adequate rest, colds and flu bugs inevitably started spreading. Part way through the camping season in 1982, Jerry came down with pneumonia. The doctor recommended three weeks of rest. Now how do you do that when there was a ten-day wilderness camp starting in a couple days, and all the equipment and supplies had to be loaded and transported? Then there was the huge job of loading up all the groceries, dishes, pots and pans, craft equipment, canoes, rifles, horses, and other paraphernalia to equip Camp Little Red for its camping season. The rest of our Camp Chestermere staff that were not needed on the wilderness camp trip would move up to Camp Little Red to help run the camps there. Recuperating from pneumonia would just have to wait. It was not surprising that, the following summer, Jerry came down with pneumonia again.

When Jerry began recruiting the next year's summer camp staff in January 1983, he challenged young people with what would become his most memorable message, "How BIG is your God? Is He big enough?" And over and over, during the next summer camping season, we faced the same challenge ourselves. Was He really able to meet our needs again that summer? Again we experienced the answer—YES! We were living proof. YES, our God was BIG—BIG ENOUGH! All in all, 1983 was a wonderful summer—excellent staff, full enrollments at both Chestermere and Little Red, some 170 counseled for salvation plus many others for other needs. And to witness again the power of Christ's blood over wrong spirits attacking campers and staff was another vivid reminder of just how great our God is! Satan is a real adversary, but God is greater than Satan!

When I drove off the camp property at the end of that camping season, the tears flowed with joy over the wonderful memories, but also with sadness at the pending goodbyes.

9

TRAINING TEAMS TO REACH KIDS

Venture Teams International

January 1984–Summer 1986

The lines are a bit blurry. When does one ministry end and another begin? With Jerry's health struggles, and the increasing family responsibilities with the addition of Jennifer to our family in February 1982, we realized we had to slow down the pace of our camp ministry involvement. We had taken on the camp directorship chiefly to provide a positive framework for us to serve as camp speakers/chaplains, sharing Christ with the campers in chapel and campfire. Now, with the expansion of both camps, it seemed that most of our energies were being absorbed again in the countless administrative details required to properly run the camps, rather than in the direct teaching of campers and the training of staff. It was time to make a tough decision and work again towards a better balance in our lives. That fall, in 1983, we resigned from the camp directorship. While we were no longer employed full-time by Camp Chestermere, we continued to speak at camps and to help train camp staff. Officially, though, we joined the staff of Venture Teams International (VTI) in January of 1984 for a one-year commitment. It ended up being almost two and a half years.

At that time, VTI was a one-year internship program in Christian ministry worldwide designed to bridge the gap between the academic input of Christian colleges, and the practical application of what had been taught. With statistics pointing to less than 10% of Bible college graduates becoming actively engaged in reaching our world, VTI was a relevant organization.

We had already been involved in some training sessions for past teams in previous years. Now our role was mainly to be responsible for training team members for children's ministries, as well as doing some travel with them in Canada, monitoring and encouraging their progress. Our background of holding teachers' workshops with CEF had equipped us to add structure and depth to the various components that already existed. We developed manuals for their children's programming and for puppetry. We expanded their visual aids resources. And we spent many hours teaching and evaluating the teams as they worked on putting together effective children's programs. In between, Jerry also helped recruit for future team members. One year he went out on some 30 various recruiting assignments.

What a privilege it was to work with many of these young adults who were newly experiencing God's faithfulness and greatness in ministry. I remember teaching one group how to focus a children's presentation for both believers and non-believers, and what specific elements you would include for each. At the end of that training class, a young man came up to talk. He was a pastor's son and had been involved in various outreaches. "Hey," he exclaimed, "that's exactly why Billy Graham's presentations are so effective. He uses those same principles!" I had never thought about that before, but he had a point!

When Jaclyn, our third child, arrived in May 1984, we had to increasingly struggle with separating our roles. We had always worked as a team in ministry. Jerry counted on me for a lot of the paper work and organizational framework to get his ideas operational. He was famous for his lists and notes on little pieces of paper. He claimed, "A short pencil is better than a long memory." There was one problem. No one else, and sometimes not even Jerry, himself, could make any sense of his little notes. Besides the minute size, there was another challenge—his dyslexia produced some amusing results. I was about the only one who could interpret those notes for him. For example, one day years later, Jaclyn and I dug out some old love letters Jerry had written me when he worked on road construction in Saskatchewan. We laughed till tears ran down our faces at such tender endearments as "Dear *Sweatheart*," and his activity reports beginning with "I've been so *bussy*." When Jerry writes notes on the bottoms of newsletters, he constantly asks, "How do you spell…?" Sometimes, when he asks me a question about something else, I just automatically begin spelling the answer! But at that time, with three little ones to care for, I could no longer devote my full time to being Jerry's around-the-clock executive assistant.

The amount of time Jerry had to be away for extended periods recruiting or travelling with teams also added stress to family life. During his absences, I would have the full responsibilities at home with the children. I would just get into a system of managing things at home on my own, and Jerry would be back. The systems would all have to change. And while it was always exciting for the children to have Daddy come home after being gone, it was harder and harder for them to see their dad drive off again. Jaclyn would stand at the front window and sob. It was a flash back for me, reminding me of when I was a kid and my dad would go away on Berean Bible College recruiting tours in spring. I remember one time when Dad was heading off, and my tears were flowing, he pulled me aside and showed me a verse in Philippians 1:29 *"For unto you it is given in the behalf of Christ, not only to believe on him, but also to suffer for his sake."* Now I had to teach my own children those same lessons of "suffering for Christ's sake."

It was while Jerry was with a VTI team in May 1986 in Sault Ste. Marie, Ontario that two notable events occurred. First, we had a giant knee-high dump of snow in Calgary on May 14 and 15—the worst spring snowstorm in Calgary's history. I was eight months pregnant with our fourth child and had the challenge of digging out our driveway.

The second event happened in Sault Ste. Marie where Jerry first met Len Lane, an insurance salesman. Len and his wife, Carol, were both active in their church. Carol was also involved in CEF in the community. Part way through the week with the VTI team ministry, Len began to share his dissatisfaction with his career focus in life. He expressed how he would love to be involved full time in some type of ministry—like Jerry was doing.

Jerry challenged him about taking the steps to change, if that was what God was putting on his heart. But to Len, raising support in his mid-40s seemed like an insurmountable hurdle. The two of them got down on their knees in that living room and gave Len's future to God.

What a thrill to see God at work in Len's life, and to find him, a few months later, moving to Calgary to join the staff of VTI. Len later served as its president for several years before moving back to Ontario to become the Vice President of Candidates and Personnel for Global Outreach Mission Inc.® Little did Jerry realize, back in that living room in Sault Ste. Marie, what big things God was about to do in Len's life, or how our lives would criss-cross with his in future years.

Jerry had some of his own future issues to settle that spring as well. VTI was asking for a long-term commitment; and Jerry wasn't sure, considering our young family, if he should be gone from home so much of the time. But what did God want? Jerry took three days to spend in prayer and fasting out in one of the empty cabins at Camp Chestermere. At the last hour of the available time, it all began to focus, and Jerry was certain he had heard from God. From the Scripture passages God directed him to, there was no doubt in his mind that he was to go back into ministry with CEF. He did not know where or how, but he was at peace. He came home, resigned from VTI, and called the national director for CEF. "Oh, that's wonderful," said Don Collins. "We want to get the work established provincially in Alberta. Would you consider staying in Calgary and being the provincial director?"

10

FAMILIAR BUT DIFFERENT

Child Evangelism Fellowship, Alberta

June 1986

I t is not usually recommended to go back to a job you have previously left; but, while this one was familiar, it was also different. We were back with Child Evangelism Fellowship, but our job this time was to get CEF of Alberta organized provincially. This role also allowed flexibility to service other ministries upon request. We could still continue to help train VTI teams and camp staff, as well as do some camp speaking and teachers' workshops on the side.

That summer, besides all the preparation involved for CEF summer outreach, we had our schedule fully booked with training sessions and camp speaking. There was just one thing that couldn't be pinned down on the schedule—the arrival time of our fourth baby. We knew when the event was *supposed* to happen; but that was no guarantee, even though our other children's births had been very close to their due dates.

Maybe it was a forewarning of things to come that this baby would not always follow suit or conform to the mold. First of all, the doctor assured us it was a boy. It wasn't, and we had to scramble to select girl names. Secondly, she was due on the 13th of June, but she did not arrive until June 18. It almost messed up our busy summer schedule! We had training with the summer camp staff for Camp Chestermere from June 23–30. Then it was on to train the CEF summer workers for Alberta and BC from July 2–11. Next we were camp speakers at Camp Okotoks July 14–20. By that time, Julie was just barely one month old! Thinking back, I wonder how I coped with keeping three older children cared for, nursing a newborn, and being involved in all of those ministry events. So much for maternity leave! But God faithfully gave strength for each day.

CEF had previously had some ministry outreaches in Alberta over the years, but nothing was organized on a provincial basis. Jerry began meeting for prayer with some people interested in reaching boys and girls. From that, a board was formed; and we began the process of setting up the constitution, bylaws, and government registration for receipting charitable donations.

Those early months were filled with challenges. We found a young lady who was willing to serve as secretary; but with her working from her home five miles away, and with having all the files in boxes, it was a logistical nightmare. What a blessing when we could rent an office on 17th Avenue SW in a building with several other Christian organizations. Desks, filing cabinets and office equipment were all donated. There was so much to do with such limited staff and resources. We wrestled again with the endless administration that was required when we really wanted to focus on front-line ministry. But we found God to be a constant source of strength. He was there when things were going great, and when things were not so great.

At last, in the fall of 1988, the government registration came through; and CEF of Alberta was official. The summer ministry that year had reached 117 clubs and 7 Vacation Bible Schools with 2555 children enrolled. Over 360 had been counseled. And we rejoiced that another full-time staff person was on board to help. The next summer, the outreach expanded to 3300 children, and again to just over 4000 children the year following. More staff members were added. We were delighted, that fall of 1990, when we could transition the provincial directorship to an experienced CEF missionary who was back from Europe and living in Alberta. Now we could concentrate our efforts on developing another facet of the ministry that we were just getting established in Alberta, a comprehensive Bible correspondence program.

Top: Gerald (Jerry) Robinson; Connie Cornell

Middle: Jerry showing who is boss; Sisters, Marilyn and Connie, 1954; Connie and Marilyn singing on CKXL 1953

Bottom: Jerry's Family: back—Jerry, Loretta; front—Shirley, Inez, David, George

Top Row: Jerry's high school grad; Connie at age 17; Wedding May 10, 1969

Middle: Missing persons event at Bible school—Connie and Jerry are on the left side; Jerry's sports car decorated in toilet tissue

Bottom: Photo for Kids Krusades promotion

Top Row: George Robinson family, 2001; Ethelwyn and Arthur Cornell; Robinson children ready to sing

Middle: Little Packages, Julie and Jaclyn

Bottom: Our family (clockwise from top)—Jerry, Jeremy, Jennifer, Jaclyn, Julie, Connie

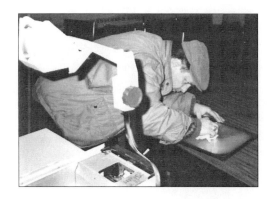

Top: Cleaning the overhead

Middle: Teaching a club at Smoky Lake

Bottom: Demonstrating counseling children with the wordless book

Top: Training teachers; Phoning camp directors

Bottom: Children's rally in Swift Current, SK; Manning our display at Grace Church, Abbotsford, BC

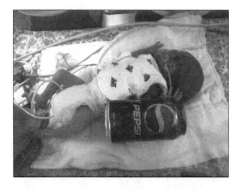

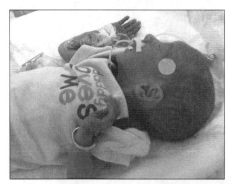

Top left: Grandson Joel had a small start

Middle: So did Katie – wearing Dad's wedding band as her bracelet

Top right: Joel and Katie, July 2011

Above: Top left—Shawn and Jennifer Switzer; top right—Jordan & Julie Cavanaugh; center—Connie and Jerry; bottom left—Jaclyn and Brett Reierson; bottom right—Jeremy Robinson

11

Raising a Family

Through all the various ministry settings with the accompanying pressures and demands of being in full-time ministry, there were the ongoing challenges of raising our own family to love and serve God.

It took a while for us to catch on to parenting—the full 27 years we had kids at home! First there was adjusting to being parents, period. After being without any children for 10 years, we really figured that all the children to whom we were ministering were the "family" God intended for us. Of course we were excited that God was actually adding to our own biological family, but there were many things to figure out. We had always worked together as a team in ministry. How would that look with family responsibilities in the mix? What would be our priorities for raising our children? What type of schooling would we opt for? How would we determine the various skills and activities our children should pursue? The list of considerations and decisions seemed endless.

The first step, before we could leave the hospital, was settling on names. We've often been asked, "Why all J's?" With us having been involved in years of children's ministries, too many names triggered bad memories. We finally decided to stick to one letter of the alphabet, and tried to select names with positive meanings. We also tried to add at least one name that was a Bible name or had Bible significance. There were times, however, that we wondered at the wisdom of our name selection when Jerry would call out all four children's names before finally connecting with the one he really wanted.

Early on, we recognized the huge responsibility we had to train our children to obey and honor their parents. Only as they learned to do that, would they begin to obey and honor their heavenly Father. As we watched them grow, it was hard to sort out what was a normal stage of development, and what was evidence of a sinful nature. We kept thinking, "What will this trait look like 10 years down the road if left unchecked?" As consistently as we could, we tried to speak once, and then have some disciplinary action if obedience was not immediate! Sometimes it was easy, and sometimes it was much more challenging. Jeremy caught on pretty quickly. I remember him announcing to the entire congregation in Dad Robinson's church as I carried him out to discipline him for his behavior, "Mama, I be good. Mama, don't spank me, I be good."

Julie, our youngest, was another story. She was quick to learn everything from her siblings and she loved music, so she knew and sang all the words of songs very early. When Julie was about 20 months old, we were visiting friends out at the west coast. We asked Julie to sing, "Jesus Loves Me."

Nothing.

We asked, "Do you know 'Jesus Loves Me'?"

She nodded.

"Will you sing 'Jesus Loves Me'?"

She got a stubborn look on her face and clamped her lips shut. Jerry took her back to a bedroom for the reinforcing "action" which included talking about the wrongdoing, praying, and spanking. All "action" was liberally sprinkled with tears from both parent and child. Back they came to the living room. Again we asked Julie to sing. Again she refused, and again she went back to the bedroom. For about an hour, the battle of wills continued. By this time we were all crying. We were desperate. Julie would come out and we would ask, "Julie, can you say 'Jesus loves me'?"

"Jesus loves me," she would repeat.

"Will you sing 'Jesus Loves Me'?"

And she would clamp her lips and glare.

It took about 1 ½ hours before Julie's will finally yielded. We were all worn out. The process had been traumatic for everyone, but Julie was noticeably more obedient after that.

Each child was unique. Jaclyn could be very stubborn, but had such a sensitive nature. Jennifer, our oldest daughter, was more of a mystery. We could spend time with her, talk and pray with her, hold her, and cry when disciplining her; but there were seldom tears from her. We wondered how to reach her. We had heard from the so-called experts that each child was different, but we were amazed at how different they actually were!

Some might have considered us to be over zealous as a result of our late start in raising children, but we really cared about being intentional in teaching them God's Word. We believed that God's Word was crucial to build into their young hearts, as that was what God had promised to bless. Each morning, we had family devotions right after breakfast, and prayed for missionaries from our missionary photo album. After supper, we spent time memorizing Bible passages until they reached club age, and then they memorized scripture verses for Awana Clubs®. Every night, we read Bible stories and prayed before bedtime. On Sunday afternoons, as the children grew older, we had them do David & Jonathan Bible correspondence lessons. With all the input they had growing up, they discovered that by the time they reached college they had a much higher level of Scriptural literacy than most of their classmates. However, knowing Scripture was just the start. It is only head knowledge, unless we live it. That is the ultimate challenge!

To help our children get involved in ministry early in life, we taught them to sing together. Julie was not quite two years old when she began singing with the others. She loved it and knew all the words. Before long they had invitations to sing at a number of places including churches, schools, seniors' homes, weddings, funerals, and at our training sessions for summer missionaries.

There were some interesting episodes along the way. Once while the kids were singing, I could hear the audience snickering even though the lyrics were not particularly humorous. I was playing piano in behind and could only see them from the back. Later I learned that Julie had stuck her hand deep inside Jeremy's pocket and was wriggling it all around during the performance. Jeremy was doing his best to ignore what was happening, but the audience was getting quite a laugh out of the antics.

Another time, Jeremy had a bad case of burp hiccups during the service. I sent him out to get a drink of water, but even that didn't help. I was praying earnestly that God would intervene as I could just imagine the outcome of the kids trying to sing with Jeremy having full-blown hiccups. The pastor was going to pray, and then the kids were on. Just as they were called, the hiccups vanished!

One year, during a Sunday School Christmas program, Jaclyn and Julie were singing a song called "Good Things Come in Little Packages." Along with the other members of their group, they were outfitted inside big, gift-wrapped boxes with just their heads, arms and legs sticking out. Part way through the song, Julie lost her balance and fell over like a little turtle on its back. She couldn't get up while encased in that big box, but that didn't faze her at all. She didn't miss a beat. She just kept right on singing until the program director lifted her back up onto her feet!

When Jeremy was ready to start school, we really deliberated over what to do. All our children had a firm grasp of phonics and could read before they began school. But what was the next step? Should we trust them to the public school system? Was the cost of a Christian school financially viable for our budget? While home schooling was an attractive alternative, for us it had three strikes against it. First, it was not readily accepted in the education system back then unless there were unique circumstances. Second, my availability to work with Jerry in ministry would have been almost totally curtailed had we opted for home schooling. And third, Jeremy would have been quite content to spend his entire life in his room with a book—or rather, hundreds of books—if we had let him. He really seemed to need the interaction and risk-taking stimulus that a school setting would offer. We were grateful for an affordable nearby Christian school with some excellent teachers to supplement our teaching on the home front.

Because of our busy ministry commitments, we chose to focus on extra-curricular activities that could be done as a family rather than running every night in every direction. Music was one choice, and each child was expected to complete Grade 8 piano before opting to quit or continue. An excellent Christian piano teacher offered to teach them for half price since we were in ministry. By having the kids go for lessons every other week, we were able to have all four take lessons for the price of one. Swimming was another choice, since we felt it was a wonderful life skill that they could even use to earn some extra income if they chose to be a lifeguard or swimming instructor in the years ahead. Jaclyn yearned to do gymnastics, but a couple lessons provided as a birthday gift had to suffice. It was not until Jeremy was in college that we discovered he had always wanted to play soccer. He still plays soccer with adult recreational leagues in the city. While we might have done a better job matching activities with our kids' individual interests, the activities we did choose seemed to be the best fit for our family dynamics at the time. We were glad that all the kids had opportunities to be involved in various sports at school, although their school was limited in what was offered.

Each spring there would be a big school track and field day. While our kids all did very well in their events, Jerry's perform-ance, one year, was not so positive. The location for the track meet was at the other end of the city; and on the way, Jerry slowed down for a school zone. After dropping off the kids, Jerry headed back home, again slowing down for the school zone. About two weeks later, a letter arrived in the mail from the Traffic Division—a ticket for going too fast in a playground zone. I told Jerry, "I know where you've been!" Apparently, when the school zone finished, a playground zone continued; but Jerry missed the playground sign and thought it was back to regular speed. The next day, we got a second letter from the Traffic Division—same thing—only this time going the opposite direction! Ouch! That was an expensive track meet!

With all the time commitments of school activities, piano practice, swimming, Awana, and singing together as a family wedged in, I often found myself ready to sit and bawl by the time supper was on the table each night. It was like taking a coke bottle and shaking it thoroughly before taking off the lid. There was really nothing wrong. It was just my stress reliever to let the "bubbles" run out of my eyes while we prayed for our evening supper. On those evenings, the kids tried extra hard to be on their best behavior during supper so I wouldn't have any further reasons to cry.

Our family fun activities were usually inexpensive. There were the early tickle games in which our kids would crawl past us till we grabbed them, one at a time, and soundly tickled them. Then we'd roll them out of the way so they could run around a circuit through the kitchen and dining room and back to the living room to wait their turn for the next tickle attack. Sometimes, in the process, they would try to steal Jerry's socks. On one occasion, Jerry did not immediately find the missing sock. It turned up a couple days later when I was preheating the oven, and a terrible smell started filling the kitchen!

Other times, we would all jump in the car and go for playground outings—about ten minutes at each of four or five different nearby playgrounds. Usually the playground trips were special highlights, except the time that Jaclyn got to the top of the stairs, lost her nerve to go down the slide, and decided to retreat back down the stairs facing outwards. Sure enough, she fell and broke her arm. She had already broken the opposite leg falling down our basement stairs. Of course, Julie, our youngest, had to keep up with Jaclyn. By the same age, she had also broken one foot and the opposite arm in different incidents. In fact, our photo album has matching pictures taken two years apart of both younger girls wearing the same green and white dress with their legs in casts. After a while, with all the sports activities, the memories of who had which injury, and when, began to blur. There were broken fingers, wrists, stitches, growing pains, Osgood Schlatter Syndrome (something weird with your knees), dislocated elbows, shin splints, and other such maladies; but they were never consequential enough to deter further active involvements.

Early family vacations were often spent taking long road trips to South Dakota to visit Grandpa and Grandma Robinson. It didn't seem to matter that six of us had to crowd into their den at night. Jerry and I slept on their hide-a-bed, two kids slept under the hide-a-bed, and the other two slept on whatever floor space was left. Sometimes Grandma would take Jeremy on safari expeditions in the nearby park. They would hunt for imaginary lions or tigers. Another time, Jeremy spent hours, with a string tied onto a stick, fishing in the little irrigation stream that trickled by the alley. It's a good thing we weren't counting on his catch for supper that night!

Later we enjoyed some memorable camping trips including destinations like Yellowstone National Park, Sandpoint Idaho, and Kananaskis Country. The latter trip happened on a July 1st weekend. On the first morning, Jerry was heading out of the tent to get breakfast started, but he could not seem to get the flap open. It was weighed down with about 1 ½ feet of fresh wet snow. To make sure we really believed his story, he brought a little snow into the tent—and into our beds! Needless to say, we decided to pack up, all the while singing Christmas carols, and head home to dry out. A couple days later, we were ready to try again—this time at a campground about an hour north of Calgary. We got our tent and campsite all set up and went to bed. In the middle of the night, I woke up and heard water closer to the tent than it should have been. Sure enough, all that snow in the mountains had melted and was flowing down the river right beside us—or rather, by this time, all around us! We hastily pulled on our clothes and did a middle-of-the-night move to another campsite that was on higher ground.

The dynamics between siblings were pretty typical. Jeremy, as the older brother, had a keen sense of responsibility and tried to make sure his three younger sisters followed protocol. Once when they were assigned to work in the yard, Jeremy climbed a tree to observe the "work site" and then gave his sisters their job instructions. They did not always appreciate his perspective! He also loved to tease—and still does! But he really cared about his sisters. Even now he initiates phone calls and arranges visits with them to keep in touch.

Jennifer was full of mischief. She was three years old when she learned to wink, but she also happened to be sporting a black eye at the time. We were in a restaurant when she decided to practice her winking skills on anyone that looked her way. She made quite an impression with her bouncy pigtails, black eye, and saucy winks! One morning, I woke up hearing sounds in the kitchen—mixing bowls and stirring spoons. Jennifer had decided she would try making ginger cookies, although she had no idea what ingredients should go in. Another day, she pretended she was dying and had Jaclyn in tears, trying to care for her. Once when we were entertaining company, it hit me that all was too quiet. We went down the hall to discover Jennifer and Jeremy had both stripped down to their underwear, poured glasses of water all over the bathroom floor, and were having a great time sliding back and forth.

But Jennifer had a protective streak about her too. The girls were playing in the back yard when, suddenly, they heard someone trying to open the back gate. Jennifer had been warned about strangers, and this was certainly someone she did not recognize. It was actually a city worker in uniform, but he figured he better back off when Jennifer came charging at him with a club in her hand. Next she raced in the back door to announce the crisis. By the time we got out to investigate, the city worker was nowhere in sight, although he had left his vehicle behind. He was likely still running!

Then there was the episode in the line-up waiting for the school bus. A school bully had been bothering Jaclyn the day before, so Jennifer was demonstrating to Jaclyn how she was going to defend her. She made a fist, wound up, swung and…SMACK! She accidentally hit Jaclyn square in the mouth, knocking out her two front teeth! Jennifer was shocked. So was Jaclyn! Both were scared about what we would say when we got the phone call from the school. We laughed! Thankfully, Jaclyn's teeth were already loose and the permanent ones were just ready to come in.

Our most treasured memories were the times we witnessed God at work in the lives of our children. We were occupied with company one evening when Jeremy emerged from our bedroom. Both he and Jennifer were tucked in our bed, supposedly heading off to sleep. Jeremy came out to announce that Jennifer wanted to ask Jesus to be her Savior from sin and that he needed help telling her what to do. Our guests were very understanding as I excused myself to go talk and pray with Jennifer.

A couple years later, it was Jennifer who was concerned for her sister Jaclyn while the girls were playing in our backyard sandbox. She explained the gospel message to Jaclyn and encouraged her to pray to receive Christ as her Savior right there.

What a joy it has been to see the progress over the years, as our children got involved in reaching out to others. All of them have worked in various capacities at children's camps. Some have been able to experience missions' trips. Some taught Sunday School, led youth groups and worship teams. They were stretched in being "lights" in university, and in their work places. It was wonderful, recently, to see Jaclyn and her husband, Brett, taking the youth sessions at a conference for Canadian Sunday School Mission staff. One of the parents wrote that her sons had looked forward to hanging out with their old friends during the conference at Three Hills since they used to live there. Instead, the boys found the sessions so helpful and encouraging, that the time with their old friends took second place. We also hear encouraging stories from Julie and her husband Jordan about some of the youth they are working with, becoming Christians and growing in their faith.

As we have seen our children grow and sometimes struggle in their own relationships with God, it is hard to wait for God's process and timing in pursuing them, in answering prayers, and in molding them after His image. We want it done NOW! But as we dedicated each one to God when they were just babies, we know that they are really His, not ours! We were only "house-parents" for a time. Is our God big enough to keep working in the lives of our adult children, their spouses, and now our grandchildren too? Even without our direct involvement? Yes, He is big enough. And we must choose to keep trusting Him.

12

GROWING KIDS YEAR-ROUND

U.B. David & I'll B. Jonathan Inc.

1987–2007

In all our years of working with children's ministries, rarely would we get to hear how kids were doing in their lives after being at a camp, Kids Krusades, or a 5-Day Club. We had no idea where most of the kids we taught ended up. Often we wondered how we could better nurture these children on an on-going basis. So many kids had little or no support from their homes. So few could be channeled into Bible believing churches. We knew that God had certainly been with children in the Bible, such as Joseph in Egypt and Naaman's maid in Syria, who had found themselves in ungodly environments. We also knew that just as babies require proper nourishment to thrive, so also new Christians needed to be nurtured and encouraged. Was there more that we could do to follow up with the kids that were being reached?

Way back in our days with CEF in Saskatchewan, we had used the Mailbox Club® lessons as part of our ministry. Each child reached was encouraged to complete the first lesson at club and then continue doing lessons by mail at home. But in spite of some incentives, many children quit after completing just a few lessons. Since that time, the CEF provincial director of Saskatchewan had developed a comprehensive follow-up program called U.B. David & I'll B. Jonathan Inc. (D&J). This program expanded the Mailbox Club to include a whole series of incentives and awards built on concepts from the lives of David and Jonathan in the Bible. It seemed to be producing some effective results in Saskatchewan.

Jerry thought maybe this was something we could implement in Alberta as well. Up to that time, one dear lady had handled the existing program of correspondence lessons for CEF of Alberta for many years; but she was at the point of giving it up because of poor health. Just then, another organization's correspondence ministry in southern Alberta decided to discontinue and asked if we would take over its 400 students. Jerry talked to the Saskatchewan director, and it was agreed to get Alberta launched with a loan of $10,000 for start-up costs. The Alberta chapter of U.B. David & I'll B. Jonathan Inc. began.

One of my aunts responded to the appeal for someone interested in a home-based Bible correspondence ministry, and we initially set up shop in their home. First it occupied one room in their basement, then more, and soon even spilled out into their garage.

About then, we received an invitation from members of Faith Chapel, a small church in downtown Calgary, to use their basement for the expanding needs of D&J. Their congregation was dwindling, and they felt this program would have a wonderful outreach to boys and girls in keeping with their mission statement. Two of Jerry's uncles had been directly involved in that little church—one in bygone years, and one more recently. In 1995, when the elderly congregation members decided the church could no longer continue, they voted to give the building, then valued at about $179,000, to D&J for the Alberta work. What a blessing! The upstairs was rented to a small church group for weekend services; and during the week, the basement was used for D&J. The rental income even covered the utilities and maintenance costs! We took apart the benches in the little basement Sunday school rooms and converted them into shelving for storing lessons. We cleaned and painted. We put in carpet to add warmth to the basement, and we upgraded wiring. And God again supplied desks, filing cabinets, tables, phone systems, and office equipment. It was amazing!

There were so many "God-stories."

One day a volunteer gave Jerry a message to call someone about some postage stamps he wanted to donate. We used hundreds of stamps in mailing lessons out to students. After some delay in connecting with the man, we learned he had a quantity of $0.45 stamps—4500 in all—to give us. At that time, regular postage had gone up to $0.47. The man kept stating that he needed a receipt for the stamps. Jerry was rather suspicious. Who would have that many stamps? Most businesses would use a postage meter for large quantity mailing.

Jerry asked the man, "Why do you have so many stamps on hand?"

He replied, "I just sold my business, and the stamps are part of the inventory. I need to show what I did with the inventory for the company books. That's why I need a receipt."

Jerry asked the next obvious question, "What kind of business was it?"

"Oh," said the man, "I had a little post office; but when my lease was up, the mall wouldn't renew it, so rather than relocate, I decided to sell it."

He went on, "I'd thought about donating the stamps to several different organizations; but when I got your newsletter telling about all the lessons you were sending out, it just seemed the Lord spoke to me and said, 'That's the place!'"

How big is your God?

Another day, Jerry got a call from Woods Gundy. The caller wanted to know if David & Jonathan had an investment portfolio. Jerry asked, "What???" He was sure they had a wrong number. D&J certainly didn't have that kind of investment wealth.

"No," the man patiently explained, "one of our clients wants to donate 200 mutual fund shares. What would you like done with them? Do you want them rolled over into David & Jonathan's portfolio, or do you want them in cash?"

It was not familiar territory for Jerry. He quickly said he would check with our chairman and get back to Woods Gundy. The chairman told Jerry to confirm with Woods Gundy that we definitely wanted those shares, but we would need to get the cash value. While we waited for the payout, the share price went up; and D&J eventually received a cheque for $9,300.

Then there was a music teacher in the area who inquired about using our building for her music recitals. We happily accommodated her on a donation basis. Some months later, we received an estate gift of $3,000. The lady had passed away, and apparently she had requested a gift of $1,500 to be sent to help the ministry we were doing. Her brother was her executor and decided to match her gift.

It seemed we were always on the lookout for better printing equipment. Jerry got a lead on a printer with six color drums, but it was owned by a print shop. Warning bells went off in Jerry's mind as usually print shops run their equipment to death. However, when he checked it out, the printer had hardly been used! It cost $35,000 new, but to us the price was $5,000 including $4,500 worth of ink. What a great provision which enabled us to update many of the D&J lessons with color!

As the work grew, all kinds of volunteers were needed: lesson markers, area coordinators, book-keepers, printers, mailing-day helpers, data entry personnel, plaque makers, and the list went on. When we decided to use oak plaques as part of the award system, we looked for someone who would make them for us. Each one had to be handmade with a metal plate mounted on the front explaining the David & Jonathan concept for that level. The plaques were attractive and were treasured by the students who earned them. But who would take on such a big task?

Jerry thought of Les Lonneberg who had recently retired from finish carpentry. He took Les out for coffee and explained the ministry of D&J and the need for a skilled volunteer to make the plaques. Les was rather non-committal. In fact, he did not say much of anything.

After a couple weeks, Les got back to Jerry about the project. He said, "Here I was, never wanting to do any more carpentry.

I was finished—goodbye tools! Then you come along and want me to consider taking this project on—for nothing! I was not impressed. But God has been speaking to me about it ever since. I've hardly slept. I know He wants me to do it." And Les did take it on for many years, making thousands of plaques. He scrounged for oak—even rescuing pieces from dumpsters. As he sanded and stained each plaque, he thought about how those plaques would be representing Jesus Christ on the walls of many homes throughout western Canada. He said he never felt more fulfilled in a job!

For twenty years we witnessed God faithfully supply funds, resources, and about 35 volunteers to continue growing the work. Both full-time and part-time staff members were added. From the 400 names we had initially received in a box, the outreach had expanded to 7,000 active correspondence students—a pretty big Sunday School class! Some 94 camps across Canada were using the lessons at that time as a follow-up program. Our D&J "answer man" was replying with Bible answers to hundreds of questions from students. It was a wonderful ministry, and we really expected to stay with it until retirement, but it was not to be. Again our nest was being stirred. Gradually we became convinced that God had some plans for us to be involved in ministry projects outside the David & Jonathan framework. After twenty years, our work there was coming to an end. Again the time had come for us to walk away and leave to others a ministry we dearly loved.

As we reflected over those years of ministry with D&J, we were grateful for so many times when we could see God's supply—so often from such unexpected sources. But there were also many struggles and many lessons for us to learn. Some of those years were the hardest years of our lives. We knew we were in a spiritual battle. When you are reaching out with the gospel message to boys and girls, facing attacks are part of the job description. We fully expected opposition to come. But sometimes the sources of that opposition took our breath away. We came away from our years with D&J feeling uncertain, battered, and bruised. We were gun shy in decision-making, lacking confidence in discerning God's mind. But there was no other hope for us except to continue anchoring in God and trying to learn the lessons God had for us in the process.

13

TRAUMA ON THE HOME FRONT

This chapter, and the next, relates some of our memories of those events we would never have chosen for part of our story. But God did. And God, in His faithfulness, used them to mold us and demonstrate His sovereignty, His love, and His sufficiency in our lives. Besides the fact that memories can play tricks on us over the years, we are also aware that our memories may not match up with the memories of others concerning the same events. But as this is a book of *our* memories, we will do our best to portray them as accurately and honestly as we can.

At first, we did not think anything of it. She was just a little late. It was June 18—Julie's sixteenth birthday. We had already celebrated with a family meal and birthday cake the previous Sunday. It did not work to have a big party on the actual date as Julie had a basketball practice after school, and Jaclyn, two years older, was in the midst of her Grade 12 diploma exams. In fact, Jaclyn was to write her chemistry final the next morning.

On each of our two older girls' sixteenth birthdays, Jerry had taken a dozen roses to present to them at the Christian school they attended as a special recognition of their day. But for her own reasons, Julie had already asked her dad not to follow that tradition for her. At the time, we figured she just did not want the attention focused on her at school.

We had decided to go pick up some pizza, which was a rare treat, as I usually made our own. But we wanted to be able to do something special on Julie's birthday. When we got home, and Julie was still not back from her basketball practice, we put the pizza into the oven and waited. And waited.

After an hour or so, we were getting past "annoyed" and into the "worried" zone. Had Julie been in an accident, or worse? I called over to Jennifer's nearby apartment to see if she had heard from Julie. Nothing. There was no answer at the school or at her friends' places. As the time ticked on, and still no sign of Julie, I suddenly got a terrible dread in the pit of my stomach. I ran down the stairs to her basement bedroom and began to look around. Sure enough, Julie's treasured belongings were all missing. We could scarcely grasp it. Julie had apparently run away from home. It was unthinkable! It was like being hit with a sledgehammer. There had been no major confrontation, no immediate family trauma, and no obvious warnings. Even Jaclyn had absolutely no foresight or inkling. But there it was—cold, harsh, and absolutely devastating!

When we finally reached her basketball coach by phone, he offered us no leads and said he did not know anything of her whereabouts. It was not until very late that night that we finally gleaned a little more information from one of the school administrators. Yes, he was aware of where Julie was, but he was not prepared to divulge that information to us. The truth began to dawn on us that others did indeed know what was happening and where our Julie was, in spite of acting as if they knew nothing. And so began a traumatic 3 ½ weeks.

Julie was a lot like Jerry—outgoing, high energy, athletic. From day one, when we took her to school and dropped her off, she was immediately surrounded by boys. It was not a big concern to us as long as there were many and not just one! She was musical and an excellent student, in spite of struggling with dyslexia issues like her father. And she was passionate about life—everything was extreme—absolutely awesome or unspeakably terrible. There was no middle ground. Her perceptions were such that she would paint events extra black or extra white, making it hard to tell what really happened.

One of Julie's dreams was to be the first female player in the National Basketball Association. She loved the game and practiced long hours on our basketball hoop that hung above the garage door. By the time she was in Grade 9, she was invited to play basketball with the high school team since they were short of players. Because Jaclyn was also on the team, we gave permission. Julie was thrilled. And she excelled. Every spare moment she was hanging out in the gym shooting baskets.

She also began to hang out with some of the girls on the high school team that were in Jaclyn's grade. Several of them were from broken homes, and some were already living on their own and driving their own vehicles. The freedom they had was very appealing to Julie and was a marked contrast from the accountability expected in our home. We held a level of standards and expectations that seemed old fashioned and rare among most of the kids, even at the Christian school. For Julie, it was conflicting. There were lots of things she was questioning; yet she did not feel she would be seriously heard if she voiced her issues at home. And she was probably right. Julie began to feel like she was one person at home and another away from home. She was probably right about that, too! It was not that she was doing drugs, or sex, or drinking, or whatever else was out there. She just wanted the freedom to be herself, and do what she felt was important for her.

In addition, there was the whole family dynamic in general. We had always encouraged our kids to do their best in whatever they did. They all did very well in school, swimming, Awana, piano and athletics and they were all high achievers. However, for Julie, other areas of life were also important—like her friends. Even though she was actually doing very well, she somehow felt that she could not live up to the "family reputation" in achievements. Yet, ironically, it was her next older sister, Jaclyn, who often felt second fiddle to Julie in basketball, in singing, and certainly in popularity at school. Even Jaclyn's classmates, especially the basketball girls, paid more attention to Julie.

But there were other issues too. Our kids had seen the stresses and strains we experienced in ministry. They saw us struggle with the issues at work and, although they knew we gave it our very best, they also saw we were imperfect parents who sometimes blew it. For example, Jerry struggled with anger management. When frustrations would mount with the various pressures, sometimes his intense nature would explode in loud, angry words. Then he would be devastated and apologize with a broken heart. We were both quite aware of our shortcomings, and were constantly bringing them to God to change us, but our "warts" were obvious to our kids.

Meanwhile, at the Christian school, Julie's coach had a huge influence on Julie as her confidant and friend. He had often asked her to be the scorekeeper for his own basketball league games outside of school. He was a good athlete, attractive, and could sing well. In fact, the graduating class had requested Julie and the coach sing a duet at their grad banquet. But from some of the stories we had heard, the coach's relationship with the girls on the basketball team was sometimes unwise, and seemed less than professional. When he had announced he would be leaving the school at the end of June to move to Nova Scotia, Julie had been devastated. But a plan was soon formulated.

Julie had shared her frustrations about her home life with her school confidants. Keeping in mind her tendency to go to the extreme, the picture she painted about home must have seemed very bleak indeed. Instead of the school officials counseling Julie towards reconciliation with her family, or attempting to verify the facts with us, or even with Jaclyn, they counseled Julie that her best option was to run away from home. She had discovered that usually, at age 16, the police and Government Social Services did not force kids to return to their homes against their will. There was even the possibility of being provided with a living allowance. That was why she waited until her 16th birthday. It also suddenly became clear why she did not want her dad bringing roses to her at school. How embarrassing that would have been to have her dad bring her roses on the very day she planned to run away from home!

We learned that Julie had been encouraged by certain school staff to bring her belongings bit by bit in her gym bag. She stored them in the coach's office until she was ready to make her move. The coach offered that Julie could travel with him by car across Canada as he headed east to reunite with his family who had already moved to the Maritimes. He suggested that spending the summer months there, far away from us as a family, would give Julie a chance to sort things out. As Julie weighed all her perceptions and the influences in her life, she was at the point of wanting to decide for herself what she was going to believe and practice in her life; and she was struggling to discern truth. So, in order to achieve the freedom and environment she thought she needed in order to really be herself, she was prepared to take drastic action on her birthday.

The next morning, with heavy hearts, we immediately sought out our pastor. He, too, had a child attending the same Christian school and had some experience with the parties involved. Bit by bit we learned more. We were to have an official visit from a social worker that afternoon. Although our older three children had all gone through the school very successfully, the school officials had called Social Services with their concerns that our home was a dangerous and unsafe place for Julie. With the pastor and Jaclyn present, the interview proceeded. We let Jaclyn answer whatever questions she could so nothing was hidden. Amazingly, God had arranged that one of the social workers assigned to meet with us that day happened to be a Christian lady that had attended the same Christian school when our son was there. The following day, we learned that Social Services had concluded our home was the very best place for Julie. They said she was doing too well in life and did not fit the typical profile of "run-a-ways." They felt it would be totally detrimental for her to go through their system.

We kept thinking we would wake up from this terrible nightmare and everything would be back to normal, but it wasn't that easy, and it didn't go away. We didn't know what else to do but humbly cast ourselves before the Lord for His mercy on us, on Julie, and on our family. Bit by bit we saw God at work in the situation.

After a few days of staying with one of her friends that was living independently, Julie's plans began to unravel. First, the Social Service Agency was not coming through for her as she anticipated. Then the coach retracted his offer of taking Julie with him across Canada. We still shudder to think of that possibility and its potential for a devastating outcome. But God, in His mercy, shut that door. Julie moved temporarily to the home of one of the school's administrators. She was a good friend with his daughter. But our efforts to communicate with her, both directly and indirectly, were rebuffed. She was still processing the skewed advice she had received.

It seemed all we could do was pray and cry, and cry and pray. Our hearts were broken. Each of us struggled to know how to handle it. Jeremy's voice broke with emotion when we called him in Lethbridge where he was attending university. He attempted to communicate with the Christian school administrators, but was very frustrated with the response. It was so difficult for Jaclyn to deal with the bitterness that threatened to overwhelm her. Besides the disappointment with her sister, Jaclyn had totally lost respect for the school staff involved. If they had

had concerns for Julie's family dynamic, why had they never asked Jaclyn about it, or her pastor, or her parents? How difficult it was for her to focus on her Grade 12 government exams. In fact she ended up dropping 20% from her classroom average on her chemistry final she had to write the day after. Every day she had to go to school with classmates who had betrayed her. Every day, for the rest of the school term, she watched Julie obviously go out of her way to avoid her, as the sisters walked the same hallways at school. And how painful it was for us to attend the school's final award ceremony and see our Julie walk back and forth to the stage without a glance in our direction.

For us, each day of uncertainty seemed like a year. One of Jerry's nephews, a Christian counselor in the States, told us that, as devastating as it was, our situation was much better than that of many parents who had no idea where their missing children were. But what were we to do? What could we do? How were we to continue with ministry responsibilities? But God was still at work. In spite of Julie enjoying the new freedoms and responsibilities of life away from home, God was beginning to challenge her in her devotions.

We were scheduled to be away for a few days, and while we were gone, both Jennifer and Jaclyn individually spent time with Julie. When we got back and walked in the door, instantly I sensed Julie was in the house. Apparently, after a visit from Jaclyn, she had come back home to pick up some more of her belongings. When she came down the steps and saw us, I burst into tears and we hugged her and hugged her. I don't remember what was said, but somehow she sensed our love and our heartbreak for our precious girl. It seemed to be a turning point. Jaclyn was to take her back to the school administrator's home where she'd been staying. But much to the consternation of the school administrator, Julie decided to pack up her stuff there and move back home. We were overjoyed. It had been 3 ½ weeks. But it was just the beginning of rebuilding trust, of hearing and communicating, and of restoration. Julie spent the rest of the summer at Camp Little Red and God continued to speak to her. Changes began to happen in her—and in us!

There was no way we could send Julie back, that fall, to a Christian school we felt had so poorly handled our situation. But our assigned public school was a concern to many district parents. After much prayer, we enrolled Julie in the boarding high school at Prairie Bible Institute. That was a hard decision, since getting away from home and wanting freedom were key factors that had precipitated Julie's running away. But God had a special surprise for us. The high school girls' dean was a fellow classmate from our own college days at Berean Bible College years before. She was an excellent dean, and was a wonderfully positive influence on Julie. No one, but the dean, was aware of what had transpired; and even she could hardly believe Julie was the same girl that had run away three months before.

Later, when Julie attended the Bible college at Prairie, she, herself, became an assistant dean to the high school girls. God had turned her 180 degrees. When some of the girls would talk to her about running away from home, she would tell them, "Don't you ever do that! I did it once and it was the dumbest thing I ever did!" Now, she and her husband work with youth in a large church setting; and she continues to mentor and impact girls who need to learn how to find their freedom in Christ. What Satan meant for evil, God meant for good.

And as we've heard where the paths led some of the other people that had impacted Julie back in high school, we are so grateful God intervened. One of the girls is already divorced. Another lived with her unsaved boyfriend for some time before finally getting married. And the administrator, whose home she had lived in, became a Buddhist and divorced his wife. How relevant is the wisdom of Psalm 1:1, *"Blessed is the man that walketh not in the counsel of the ungodly, nor standeth in the way of sinners, nor sitteth in the seat of the scornful."* How critical to base our life choices on God's principles and God's ways.

Incidentally, Julie did end up getting a bouquet of roses from her dad for her sixteenth birthday—just a few weeks late—the day after she moved back home.

All during grade school and high school, our oldest daughter, Jennifer, had prayed for a good friend. Sometimes she would find someone she thought was compatible, but it just did not last. At Peace River Bible Institute, she did well in her studies, but finding good friends was another challenge. She had a line-up of guys— mostly not the kind we would have chosen—that were competing for her attentions. They were difficult years; and Jennifer struggled to find her way, sorting out her own values and beliefs. With some starts and stops, she completed the two-year program.

Growing up, she always loved visiting her uncle's farm; and when she got a landscaping job after Bible school, it seemed like a fit. Before long, she had her own crew, was driving a bobcat and other equipment including a one-ton truck and trailer through the city, and learning lots. But the company management's ethics were very questionable, and Jennifer decided to quit. One of her co-workers, Shawn, had family in Ontario and wanted to move back home. With an offer of a place to stay, Jennifer decided to go east, too, and explore more of Canada. We all shed tears that November 2003 as she packed up her apartment and we hugged her goodbye.

The next November, she came home for a visit. It was great to see her and she brought pictures of some of the landscaping jobs she had worked on. Shawn's grandmother, a sweet Christian lady, phoned her a couple times while she was here, just to make sure she was coming back!

Then, in February 2005, we tried off and on all one weekend to get through to Jennifer by phone. Finally, on the following Monday evening, Jennifer called back. We told her we had been trying to reach her to see how things were going, and she told us that she had been away.

"What were you doing?" we asked.

"I got married," was the reply. "Shawn and I went winter camping on our honeymoon."

We didn't even know she was dating him!

It was a typical "Jennifer" thing to do, as she would never have been comfortable being the center of attention at a big wedding. And since they were just planning a very simple wedding in the pastor's home, they didn't think it was worth our cost to fly out there for a 20-minute ceremony. So, they decided to make it a surprise. Not even Shawn's family knew.

After picking ourselves off the floor, we offered our congratulations to them both, and asked the Lord to help us build good relationships with our first son-in-law and his family. But it was still hard, not getting invited to attend your oldest daughter's wedding.

Since then, God has allowed us to have several visits back and forth. Jaclyn and I went out to visit first—56 hours one way on the Greyhound bus, and then back again! What an adventure! We discovered a hundred and one ways how not to sleep on the bus! During our visit, Jerry was scheduled to fly out to a conference in Ontario. He was able to borrow a car, and drive about five hours up to surprise Jennifer on Father's Day. Shawn was in the shed and saw this stranger sneaking up his steps and right into the house. Shawn followed, with his fists clenched, ready to confront the stranger. "What do you want?" Shawn demanded.

Jerry said, "I'm your father-in-law. Come and give me a hug." What a way to meet!

Another time, Jerry was asked to attend the National Child Evangelism Fellowship Canadian conference. Guess where it was being held—right in Jennifer's nearby town! How special it was that God arranged that location!

One fall, some of our supporters provided Jennifer with travel points so she could come home on a surprise visit. At least it was a surprise to Jerry! It was quite a job for me to keep his calendar clear for the week that Jennifer was coming. People would call and set up appointments with him, and as soon as he went out the door, I would call them back and cancel or reschedule the appointments. When I saw Jennifer coming up the walk to ring the bell, I opened the door, talked briefly, and then called to Jerry to get off the phone as someone wanted him at the door. He was not too pleased about curtailing his call, but when he got to the door and saw Jennifer, he was absolutely speechless! A rare occasion indeed! Jerry being speechless, that is!

What a special Christmas we had in 2009 when Shawn's dad, step mom and brother all came out with Shawn & Jennifer to spend the holidays with us. What assurance we have knowing that God continues to work in their lives, even on the other side of the country!

In 2008, we were thrilled to find out that Brett and Jaclyn, our middle daughter, were expecting their first baby, due in early March 2009. This was to be our first grandchild; and, while it took Jerry some time to warm up to the idea of being a grandparent, even he was beginning to get excited. Jerry just figured he was not quite ready for grandparenting. That was only for old people!

As a nurse out at the Three Hills hospital, Jaclyn was so happy she would be able to have the homey atmosphere of a rural hospital for their delivery. Her pregnancy had been a little difficult with nausea, but otherwise things seemed to be progressing well. Then, in early December, she began getting migraines that started in the middle of the night. She had suffered from the occasional migraine in the past, and others were also complaining of suffering with migraines with the changeable weather patterns that December. The headaches, themselves, did not immediately trigger a warning. And having swollen ankles is a pretty common malady, too. But she was also experiencing some severe abdominal pain.

It was the morning of December 8, 2008 that Jaclyn called me saying she hardly recognized herself because her face was puffy. I am no medic; I did not even take biology in high school. But right away the thought came, "You need to get your blood pressure checked." Since she did not know if she was up to walking down town on her own to take her blood pressure at the local pharmacy, she waited until Brett came home from work. She got concerned when the pharmacy blood pressure machine did not register, so they headed for the hospital to check it there.

That began a whirlwind of activity. That evening, her blood pressure soared from 150/94 to 230/130 before finally responding to drug therapy. Her headache was excruciating and to top it all off, she had an allergic reaction to morphine. Late that evening, Jaclyn was rushed by ambulance to the Foothills Hospital in Calgary. They had already begun steroid injections which were to be administered 24 hours apart to help the baby's lung development. The goal was to stave off early delivery for 48 hours, if possible, to get the maximum benefit from the injections. Jaclyn was just at 28 weeks gestation.

Then came a phone call from Brett. He was on his way to Calgary in his own vehicle behind the ambulance and had hit a deer. While the car was still drivable, the insurance company later considered it a write-off. We were so thankful his life had been spared, but why did it have to happen at such a crisis point for Jaclyn?

At Foothills Hospital, we waited through the long night with Brett as the medical staff worked to stabilize Jaclyn's condition. Emails and phone calls were made to request prayer. We were overwhelmed at the care and support of people around the world as we together laid our daughter and the baby into God's hands. I knew there were worse things than having a daughter and grandbaby in heaven. But was that God's plan for this young couple training for the mission field? God's ways are not our ways and I was challenged to trust Him no matter what the outcome.

Another day came and went, along with other family members and pastors. The severe high blood pressure had triggered a rare complication known as Hellp Syndrome which, simply put, means vital organs shutting down. Her condition was critical. That night, Jerry and I read together from *Streams in the Desert* by Mrs. Chas. E. Cowman:

> Are there not some in your circle to whom you naturally betake yourself in times of trial and sorrow? …They have watched the slow untwisting of some silver cord on which the lamp of life hung. They have stood by…noon sunsets…but all this has been necessary to make them the nurses, the physicians, the priests of men…. Do not fret, or set your teeth, or wait doggedly for the suffering to pass; but get out of it all you can, both for yourself and for your service to your generation, according to the will of God.

And right across the page, these words:

> It is comforting to know that sorrow tarries only for the night; it takes its leave in the morning. A thunderstorm is very brief when put alongside the long summer day. 'Weeping may endure for the night but joy cometh in the morning.'

How had God arranged for the author to write those pertinent lines so many years ago? It was as if the writer knew just what we would be going through right then.

By the next morning, time was running out. The doctors could wait no longer. Jaclyn was losing her vision, her kidneys were failing, and her blood quality was quickly deteriorating. On December 10, some 36 hours after the first injection, an emergency C-section was performed. During the surgery, Jaclyn had to be revived twice. Her blood pressure had plunged to under 50/30 within seconds. In the midst of all the chaos, a perfectly formed little boy was born, weighing 1 pound 14 ounces.

Joel Daniel Giuseppe ("Joseph" in Italian) Reierson had a name almost longer than he was. From his head to his belly button was the length of a Pepsi can. But as his two-month stay in the Neonatal Intensive Care Unit progressed, he continued to beat the health issues common to premature infants. Joel was doing remarkably well.

Brett and Jaclyn stayed with us during the time Joel was in hospital. As I cared for them all during that time, I realized what a toll the crisis had taken on both Brett and Jaclyn. Brett had to hunt for a different vehicle and was also trying to study for his airplane mechanics license, but concentration was a challenge. Jaclyn's system was recovering from a major trauma, besides the usual adjustments of being a new mom and healing after the C-Section. She also had to endure the challenging process of pumping breast milk every three or four hours around the clock to keep the hospital supplied with milk for Joel. And there were the daily hospital treks to spend time with Joel. It was towards the end of the two months that, one day, Jaclyn announced, "I'm back!" She was finally starting to feel "normal" again. How grateful we were for God's mercy. It was later that we became even more aware of how God had His hand on Jaclyn during that time. Jaclyn had been transferred to the best hospital in Alberta for dealing with her pregnancy complications. The unit's nurses said she had the best surgeon possible, and Joel's doctor was the chief of staff for the hospital he was in!

Two years later, Jaclyn was pregnant again. She had received lots of conflicting advice about the likelihood of experiencing a similar crisis during the third trimester of another pregnancy. At least she was under the care of an excellent specialist with awareness of her previous pregnancy history. This time she made it to 30 weeks before more rare complications of high blood pressure resulted in another premature C-section. Little Katie Hannah Renee Reierson arrived at 2 pounds, 1 ounce, and amazed the medical staff with her progress. She was discharged from the hospital at 3 pounds, 15 ounces! The parting words to Jaclyn from one of the NICU nurses were, "If you ever start thinking about getting pregnant again, go get yourselves a dog instead!"

When I was growing up, I would sing songs with words like *"When all my labors and trials are o'er"* and *"A shelter in the time of storm."* Such words really had no significant meaning for me. I had had an uneventful life up to that point. Trials and storms—at least things more significant than acne or bunions!—belonged to someone else, somewhere else. But how wonderful, now, to have experienced a God who cares during the traumas of life, a God who is sovereign, who is big enough! He was there when we lost my dad suddenly in the middle of a camping season, and when my mom fell down a full flight of basement steps while visiting her sister, never fully recovering before she passed away two months later. He was there when people we loved failed morally, when divorce invaded our family circle, and when news came of the tragic death of Ron Royce, Jerry's brother-in-law, killed in a plane crash. Ron was a chief flight instructor for Moody Aviation and had trained hundreds of missionary pilots.

That fateful day, he was training another pilot heading to Africa. At those times of trauma, when Satan would taunt us with, "How big is your God?" we learned that we could still affirm with certainty, "He is big enough!"

14

TOUGH TIMES IN MINISTRY

Our children used to sing a little song about Bible characters, like David, Daniel, and Daniel's three Hebrew friends, all of whom faced tough challenges. The chorus went like this:

> *Run if you want to, run if you will,*
> *But I came here to stay.*
> *When I fall down I'm going to try to get up*
> *Cause I didn't start out to play.*
> *It's a battlefield, brother, not a recreation room,*
> *It's a fight and not a game.*
> *Run if you want to, run if you will,*
> *But I came here to stay.*

That song was chosen to be an encouragement for CEF summer missionaries who were being trained to head out and teach 5-Day Clubs. And we prayed that the words would also impact our own children in years to come. But how many times *we* were the ones who needed to be reminded of those words—*"It's a battlefield, brother, not a recreation room!"*

We were numb. We could not believe it. We had just gotten off the phone from our supporting church in Abbotsford, BC: they were requesting we come out immediately to meet with the leadership there. They had heard some ugly rumors and wanted some answers.

As we wept and prayed together that night, we were directed to the reading in *Streams in the Desert* for February 1—*"This thing is from me"* (1 Kings 12:24). The commentary was absolutely pertinent for our situation that day, including these words:

> Are you in difficult circumstances, surrounded by people who do not understand you, who never consult your taste, who put you in the background? This thing is from Me. I am the God of circumstances. Thou camest not to thy place by accident, it is the very place God meant for thee.
>
> Are you passing through a night of sorrow? This thing is from Me.

Our committee had granted us a much-needed three-month sabbatical. We were grateful for the time to reflect, restore, and refocus. But instead of a rest, we were hit with the full fury of the storm.

A few months earlier, we had been so thankful for some new co-workers joining in the ministry. They had sold their property and moved to Calgary to help manage the ministry's office. But it was not long before some problems surfaced. It seemed that the new people were slighted with small, everyday tasks. They considered it demeaning to be asked to oversee jobs like sorting the sizes of rubber bands or paper clips. And when Jerry checked to make sure things had been taken care of, the monitoring was not welcomed.

There was another issue—money management. Although the new couple had first come to us as volunteers, they soon began to expect reimbursement, especially when they saw others on staff receiving salaries from support accounts. Coming from a secular work environment, they found it hard to understand how charitable organizations operated on donated dollars. They were used to having access to generous expense accounts; and, if they were required to eat out on business for the mission, in their minds, the cost was largely irrelevant. They were also irritated when Jerry would remind volunteers to turn off lights and to shop hard for the best value in office supplies. To them, Jerry's tight rein on spending was not a matter of wise stewardship, but rather just a sign of Jerry's stinginess and a fixation on hoarding financial resources.

One day that fall, we held an open house for the ministry. Volunteers manned different stations, explaining the work to visitors. A little box was set out for donations towards a project. When the event was finished, and most people had gone home, Jerry saw the box still sitting there. Since another group shared the building, we took the box into the office, opened it, and counted the money—about $53 worth. Then we sealed it in an envelope and placed it in the special place for the volunteer who did deposits. It was not until sometime later that we heard the rumor circulating, *"Jerry and Connie took the money home. How do we really know how much was in that box? Is some missing?"*

There were also questions about a donation that had come in from one of our supporting churches. For years, that church had pledged a specific amount for our support from their missions' fund. In addition, some individuals also designated monies towards our support; and the church kindly handled those gifts, adding the amount to their support, and sending it on to the ministry. Someone else always opened the mail and made the deposits according to the designation. However, while we were on our sabbatical, our new co-worker opened the mail one day. He saw the donation from the church and the various individuals and assumed that part of the donation should have been going into the general fund account, not to our support account as it had in the past. Instead of checking with the church, again he voiced his suspicions, *"Those Robinson's must be misappropriating funds!"*

We could not believe our ears when the rumors started to get back to us. Our kids at first thought it was funny, as they had seen me return to the grocery store and give back extra change. And we all knew that Jerry, of all people, had the gift of giving. He was quite happy with $5 in his pocket; but when he went off to visit Bible colleges, I would usually send him a little surplus for emergencies. He seemed to have an uncanny knack of finding some student or couple struggling financially, and would give his money away. Needless to say, we were devastated at the insinuations. Mistrust and bitterness flourished.

It was at that point that we got the phone call from the church in Abbotsford. When we arrived there a few days later, we shared our hearts, our struggles, and our devastation. Others had also spoken to the church on our behalf. How grateful we were for the wisdom and support of that missions' board. What an encouragement they were!

But how different was the atmosphere at the little church we were attending in Calgary. The new co-workers were good friends with the pastor couple at that time. It was really awkward, our family sitting on one side, with the other couple on the opposite side. We felt like we were being treated as lepers. Our children felt ostracized. We finally met with the pastor and told him we felt it would be wise for us, and for the sake of the other couple, to take a recess from the church for a three-month period to allow time for things to be resolved and for healing to take place. During part of that time we would be out of the country anyway.

When we arrived back in the country and were going through our mail, we discovered a letter of dismissal from the church, signed by the pastor. Even our son, Jeremy, who was old enough to be a member at that time, also received a letter of dismissal. We were shocked. When we called one of the two church elders, a Wycliffe missionary, to ask about it, he could not believe it. It had happened without his knowledge. And he discovered that we were not the only ones to have been singled out and dismissed. Apparently there were a number of serious concerns about the way several other people and situations within the church were being handled there. Shortly after that, the pastor abruptly resigned.

But the upheaval within the ministry was a bigger setback. We ended up losing several staff members and volunteers. It would take a long time to restore trust. We struggled with how to handle the rumors and defend the truth. Should we say nothing and let the Lord protect our honor? It was one thing if it just reflected on our personal reputation. But when it reflected upon the ministry, that was a greater concern. We were experiencing the spiritual battlefield at a new level. We became increasingly aware that *"the battle is the Lord's"* (1 Samuel 17:47). Our best efforts count for nothing *"in the flesh."* The work was God's. We were God's, and His ways are not our ways. While we were reeling from all this turmoil, Satan had more surprises, this time in the physical realm.

It seemed like it was a dangerous thing to be a ministry volunteer. One after another, our volunteers were getting knocked out of service—one breaking a leg in a car accident, another breaking both wrists, another falling on the street. I was not immune either. I slipped on ice and broke both bones just above my right ankle. It took a plate, six screws, and months of recovery; but how grateful I was when I could walk again! And how grateful Jerry was that he did not have to do all the grocery shopping anymore. I had even drawn him a coded map of the grocery store, but unbeknownst to me, the grocery store went through an overhaul just then, and everything was rearranged!

Also, for a period of time, it seemed like we were targets for car accidents—one after another. Jeremy was hit by a drunk driver: our van got T-boned by another driver sliding down an alleyway and into the traffic. Then I got backed into while sitting at the gas pumps. Even though no one was seriously injured, and even though the accidents were not our fault, they still ate up time and money getting the repairs done. We used to tease our auto body repairman that the tenth repair should be for free!

Perhaps the hardest blow was the painful conclusion to our involvement in a ministry we had loved. We had initiated the work in this area, watched it grow, worked with a wonderful team of volunteers, and saw many lives growing in the Lord. We had recognized it was time to begin turning over the reins to younger people, planning to mentor them through the next few years. But before that could happen, we sensed we were being set aside. God had other things in mind to teach us.

Over the years there had been lots of changes in how the ministry functioned here. At first, together with our working committee, we had the freedom to develop and fund the work as God provided. But gradually, the control of our practical operations, our vision, finances and personnel had been taken over by the president in another province. Our committee was frustrated with the lack of movement or answers forthcoming from headquarters to our concerns for future leadership. Instead, Jerry was asked to vacate the position of director for Alberta, and take on a national role. That meant moving out of the Calgary office, and setting up his office at home. It was not the smooth transition we had envisioned and it was sad to see our area committee dismantled, but Jerry set to work in the new role.

After the initial bustle of getting the new department organized and operating, Jerry found there were slack periods in the year. Contacts for the ministry expansion in that department could not be made 365 days of the year. We had already had some involvement with another mission project in Central America (Chapter 16), so we made the suggestion that we share our time with both ministry organizations. That was not well received.

As we struggled with the dynamics, Jerry kept being reminded, *"Be still and know that I am God"* (Psalm 46:10). So we stayed. And we stayed. For two years we pressed on, seeking to finish well and to be faithful. We did not want the ministry to suffer because of different leadership philosophies. It was a great work. It was God's work, and not ours. But more and more we were feeling marginalized. And more and more, Jerry was wondering what was next.

A dream and a random reading settled it. Jerry dreamt one night that he was attending a Child Evangelism Fellowship banquet. The emcee came to Jerry with news that the speaker had been involved in an accident and would not be able to make it. Would Jerry speak? Knowing what it takes for Jerry's preparation, it was a big challenge. But Jerry said he would try to fill in. As he ate his meal, he desperately prayed, asking God what he should say. It began to come to him. *"Abraham went out...not knowing whither he went."* Well, that was two points. But everyone knows a sermon needs three! Just then the emcee introduced Jerry and called him to the platform. "God," he prayed frantically, "I need another point!" At that moment, the third point popped into his mind..."*and God was with him.*" With that, Jerry woke up. When he told me his dream, I acknowledged that maybe God was speaking to us, but...well...it was just a dream!

A few days later, Jerry woke up in the middle of the night. For months we had been seeking God's confirmation—to stay or to go. It really did not matter to us. We just wanted God's will. Jerry prayed again, and asked God to show him from His Word. He told the Lord, "I know You can speak to me from anything You want to use."

Jerry opened his Bible to the book of Amos and began to read—chapter 1, chapter 2, chapter 3... By the time he started into chapter 8, he was getting desperate. "Lord," he prayed again, "please show me what to do." Jerry had reached the bottom of the column in his Bible with these words, *"Then said the LORD unto me..."* At that moment Jerry had a deep impression that God's answer was at the top of the next column of print. And there were the words, *"The end is come..."*

The next morning we both sensed that God was indeed closing that chapter of our lives, so we sent in our resignation. We still planned to help out for several months over the busy summer season, and we did all we could to turn things over well. But with no definite plans for the next step in ministry, it really was a bit scary!

Now, as we think back on some of those difficult valleys in ministry, we see God's hand in shaping us and in using all those circumstances as tools in our lives. While our flesh would scream that it just was not fair, our spirits acknowledged that God had designed our classroom deliberately and with great purpose in mind. He knew exactly what we needed to learn, and how best to teach us. Now we could sing from experience the little song by William G Hathaway that we taught years before at camp:

> *Trust in the Lord and don't despair*
> *He is a Friend so true,*
> *No matter what your troubles are,*
> *Jesus will see you through.*

15

Out and Beyond

Global Outreach Mission Inc.

Summer 2007—

We could hardly believe we had actually resigned. After months of thinking about that moment, and delaying, and reevaluating, and praying, and praying again, we had cut the strings. That morning, after clicking the computer's "send" icon on our letter of resignation, we looked at one another and wondered what was next. Jerry was sixty-two. Who would want him to come on board at that age?

Briiiinggg. The phone rang that same day. It was Len Lane from Global Outreach Mission Inc.® (GOM). After serving as the Executive Director for Venture Teams International for several years, Len was now the Vice President of Candidates and Personnel for GOM. He said they had just been talking about us at the GOM home office and really wanted us to consider coming under their umbrella with wide-open options for ministry. He didn't know we had just resigned that morning, and we didn't tell him that day. But our hearts were stirred. Was this of God? As we prayed and contacted supporting churches as well as individuals to serve as references, we sensed a very positive affirmation.

The main job description was to help mobilize people and resources for "around the globe" ministries, both career and short-term projects. We would serve as reps for GOM in western Canada. One of our biggest assets, at this point in life, was the many contacts we had made over the years of ministry in western Canada. Jerry was excellent in relating to young adults and challenging them about their lives. In addition, we could continue to help facilitate the development of a Costa Rican project we had been involved in (Chapter 16). We were also free to network with other organizations for ministry projects—camp speaking, people care, church involvement, and so on. This environment of generosity in ministry connections under GOM was refreshing for us in contrast to the restraints we had sensed in our previous ministry.

But there was no set framework for our weekly schedule. After being so heavily involved in running ministry "factories," there was a huge vacuum. It was timely that our kids had joined forces and given Jerry a new recliner chair for Father's Day that summer! For hours he sat in that chair and spent time with God. How should he be developing this new ministry "thing" or whatever it was? What should he be doing? Gradually, as he got quiet before the Lord, he began to catch on—God wanted him to *be like God*, not to just *work for God*. He told God he had not had time to become like God before—he was too busy working for Him. Now God had given him time.

Jerry began to ask questions like "What really is important to God? What are His priorities for our lives?" It is so difficult to keep perspective in the rush of life. We get so caught up with activity—even good activity—that we tend to miss what is dear to God's heart and what His plan is for reaching a lost world.

As Jerry mulled over those questions, he read in John 5:19 that Jesus did nothing but what the Father told Him to do. But what did that look like? It was really quite basic. Jesus trained His disciples and then commissioned them to go and disciple others. Right from the beginning, it was a pattern God established by arranging people in families so children could be discipled by parents, and younger children could be discipled by older siblings. In the New Testament, God set believers into church units so the older ones could train the younger. We began to realize that whatever shape our days took, we really needed to focus on God's priorities in our lives.

As we began to grow into our new role with GOM, Jerry started to enjoy the new freedom. He no longer carried the weight of directing and running organizations. Now he could concentrate on being discipled himself and discipling or mentoring other individuals either in regular time-frames, or woven throughout our other roles.

So it was that, that over the next few months, Jerry found his days mostly invested in these three main facets: mentoring, ministry, and mobilizing.

MENTORING

To get started with GOM, I suggested that we could do some visiting of various churches in order to connect with people and maybe make some contacts for the mission. Jerry agreed. The first Sunday, we visited a nearby church; and afterwards, Jerry ran into Bob*. He had not seen Bob for years.

"Hey, how're you doing, Bob?" Jerry asked.

"Oh fine, just fine," said Bob.

"How are your wife and family doing?" he asked further.

"Fine. The kids are all grown up now."

Suddenly, Jerry had this gut feeling. He looked Bob straight in the eye and said, "Bob, how are things really going? If they are going fine, that's good, but I want to know the truth. I care about you."

"Do you really want to know?" asked Bob.

"Yes, I really want to know."

"Well, it was the worst couple weeks of my life," said Bob. He went on to explain. His wife had been gone for several days and had just notified him she was planning to get a lawyer and file for divorce. His business was falling apart. And he only communicated with one of his five kids. He had not talked to one of them for twelve years.

The church foyer was not exactly the right place to have an in depth conversation, so Jerry gave Bob his card and said, "If you want to meet for coffee, give me a call this week."

"I'd like that," said Bob, "I'll call you tomorrow."

Monday came and went—and Tuesday—and Wednesday. Still no call. On Thursday I said, "Why don't we pray that if God wants Bob in your life, he will call today?" So we prayed.

That afternoon, Bob called. He had misplaced Jerry's business card and just found it. He was wondering if Jerry could meet him after work. So began a weekly connection with Bob—

---

* Names have been changed to protect personal identities.

hearing his struggles, praying together, and then eventually beginning a regular mentoring and discipleship time. In spite of the overwhelming dynamics of Bob's life, one day he told Jerry, "My business is under new management."

"Oh," said Jerry. What do you mean?

"Well," said Bob, "look at that sign above the door."

Jerry looked. There was no sign that he could see.

"It says 'This business is owned by God'," explained Bob.

What special times they have had together, being honest and growing in the Lord. Recently Jerry asked Bob what their weekly time has meant to him. He shared, "I'd sooner cut off my right index finger than miss our time together." And now, Bob is discipling other men!

Not long after Jerry began meeting with Bob, the phone rang. It was Sam*. We had gone to Bible college with Sam, but hadn't crossed paths very often over the years. The last time had been several years previous when Jerry and Sam had seen one another in a parking lot. They had visited briefly, and Jerry had given him his calling card.

Now Sam wanted to meet for coffee at Tim Horton's. Jerry thought, "Maybe he thinks I am still with David & Jonathan Inc. and wants to make a donation."

They met, and after the preliminary chitchat, Sam got right into it. He said he had thought of calling Jerry many times, but never could bring himself to do it. He still carried Jerry's business card. Now he was desperate. And the story began to pour out.

Sam had just gotten busted downtown Calgary in the red-light district. He had picked up an under-cover cop. His said his first sexual encounter happened while he was attending Bible college. He had gone downtown and picked up a prostitute. Since then, he had continued that lifestyle in thousands of encounters with prostitutes for forty years. Now the justice system was "throwing the book at him" because of his job as a health care professional. He should have known better! He knew he was in big trouble.

In spite of being shocked at the story he had just heard, Jerry began to laugh. He said, "Sam, isn't it wonderful that God loves you so much he had you caught! He wants to show you there is another way to live."

Jerry went on to explain, "We all have the ugly old *self-life*. Yes, we have been saved from our sin, but we need to be saved daily from our self."

Sam shared that all his life he had wished for someone to mentor him in his Christian walk. He was eager for Jerry to begin discipling him.

One by one, God kept putting people into our lives, hurting people from all walks of life: a pastor, a businessman, a retired man, and Chad*—a man living on disability pension.

Chad was a fellow who had come to volunteer for David & Jonathan. At first he bristled when Jerry had talked about the gospel message in the Bible correspondence lessons. Chad made it plain that he would come down to help, but he did not want to be preached at.

Even after we had switched to working with GOM, Jerry would often still go down to Tim Horton's for lunch with the men on Wednesdays. He wanted to continue connecting with

Chad since that was the one day Chad would be volunteering. Sometimes one or two other men would join them. It was a great opportunity to share, and Jerry would relate about the things God was doing in His life.

One day, Chad announced he was now going to a church in downtown Calgary. A few months later, he said he had joined the choir. Then one day he asked for prayer. He needed a part-time job, just a few hours a week, since he was unable to work longer. Two weeks later, he came back excited. He had a job that was just right for him. Jerry said they should pray and thank God for answering.

Then there was the Wednesday Jerry asked Chad if he would like to say the blessing for the food.

"Uh...okay," said Chad with some hesitation. With his eyes wide open, he began:

"Dear God, this is Chad here. We're at Tim Horton's and we're just here having the soup deal. Jerry's on my left and Ken is over here on my right. Uh...it is partly sunny out today, and partly cloudy. We've been over at the office working for you, but we just came here for lunch. Uh...oh yah...thanks for this food we've got."

There was a long pause, and then Chad asked, "How do you end this thing anyway?"

What a refreshing prayer from a man just getting started with God!

MINISTRY

Besides ongoing mentoring opportunities, occasionally we had the privilege of doing some direct children's ministry again.

We had been out of that facet of ministry for some time, so we weren't sure how children would take to presentations that were not packaged with the latest technology. The coordinators of one family camp said they had specifically requested our style of sessions for their children's ministry because they wanted substance—not just entertainment. Some of the parents came to observe and shared afterwards that what we gave was exactly what they wanted for the children. We were encouraged. And we were reminded that God promises to bless His Word, not all our packaging and presentation devices.

Then one of our long-time supporters called us from northern Alberta. Would we come and teach a week of VBS in two little towns up there? We agreed.

We had just rounded the corner and there, in the valley, was the picturesque little town of Smoky Lake with its quaint Orthodox churches. But immediately we sensed the spiritual darkness. We were to have VBS in the parks of each town, one in the morning at Smoky Lake, and the other in the afternoon at Vilna, a town some 45 minutes' drive away. But where were the children? When we drove through the towns, we did not see any children out playing anywhere. We began to wonder if anyone would show up, and on the first day, we began with just three kids in one town and five in the other. The children who did come came from the farms. The Lord reminded us *"Christ needed to go through Samaria...for just one woman at the well."*

As the week went on, 21 children came in all, and they absorbed the truths like sponges. Few knew even the common Bible stories. On the last day, we quizzed the children on their memory verses. We said just one key word, and they instantly jumped up to quote the complete verse. What a joy I had to counsel some of those children. Meanwhile, Jerry was talking with an adult helper. She had tears in her eyes on the Friday after VBS. She said that now, for the first time, she really knew she was saved and on her way to heaven.

On the first Sunday in Smoky Lake, we met a native man named Harvy, and his family. At first, he was hesitant to open up. We asked him if he knew of Billy Jackson, a former Berean grad who had worked for many years with First Nations peoples in northern Alberta. Harvy's face lit up. He said, "That's how I became a Christian. He explained that Billy Jackson had arranged for special meetings and a pastor from Calgary had come up to speak—Pastor Bill Laing.

I said, "When I was growing up, he was my pastor!"

"Well," Harvy said, "he wasn't the one that actually led me to the Lord. It was another man who became a missionary to Brazil. His name was Dale Snyder.

"We know him, too!" we grinned. "We'll try to call him when we get home and tell him we met you."

"Yes," said Harvy, "you tell him that drunk old Indian he led to the Lord 45 years ago is still walking with the Lord."

And Dale was delighted when we called him about Harvy! We may never know the rippling effect as people go out and faithfully share the gospel.

Later that week we tried to visit Harvy at his home in the country. Twice, we got lost. Twice, God led us to ask directions at farmhouses—exactly where people lived that knew Harvy. In fact, they were people we had met in church on the previous Sunday. And Harvy was thrilled we came for a visit.

Mobilizing

Jerry's official task with GOM was to mobilize or recruit people interested in short-term or long-term career missions' opportunities around the world. The usual expectation is to find organized settings such as mission conferences at churches and Bible colleges where we could set up a display and interact with individuals to create interest in our mission and its opportunities. But Jerry has a fat wallet—not filled with money, but with calling cards for various mission agencies. His heart is to see people find the right connection for them. He's not very good at just recruiting for *his* organization: instead he recruits for *all* the organizations! If individuals have had little or no experience in ministry but want to work with kids, Jerry might encourage them to spend a summer serving at camp, or as a summer missionary for Child Evangelism Fellowship. If they are interested in arts and drama, he might connect them with Venture Teams International for their one-year outreach teams.

That's what happened on a trip to Peace River Bible Institute. One of Jerry's student hosts, David, welcomed him with a little card and his own clean towels, set out for Jerry to use while sharing his room. David was a third year student, the academic type, serious, and with a heart for other nationalities. He was capable, but hesitant. One evening, Jerry talked with David. He told him how he got started in ministry—the little baby steps that taught him to trust God. He shared how God switched him from road construction to children's ministry. He shared some of the principles for true success that Daniel demonstrated in Scripture. And then Jerry challenged him to visit the missions' booths and pick up brochures. David did.

Next, David called his folks in Abbotsford and talked almost two hours about the things God was challenging him with at the conference. He really liked languages, so Jerry suggested he should go talk to the Wycliffe representative. What an encouragement, the following day, to see David sitting with Darrell, the rep from Wycliffe, and sense his excitement that God might even use him to reach a lost world!

Jerry met Venus at Bible School in Lac La Biche years ago. Her whole countenance portrayed defeat and discouragement. Jerry sat down with her and began to chat. Bit by bit she shared her story. She had witnessed her mother's murder at the hands of her stepfather while she and her half-sisters had crouched in terror under the kitchen table. She had seen the futility of a drinking lifestyle and the resulting tragedy that happened so commonly among her native people. She had lived on the streets of downtown Calgary, from one bar to another. But Venus could not get out of her mind some of the scripture truths shared by a friend that had attended a Sunday School as a child. By a miracle of God's grace, Venus had eventually chosen to receive Christ as her Savior.

When she arrived at KeeWayTin Bible School, Venus was quickly overwhelmed. Everything was so new. Her past still haunted her. There was so much pain, and the tattoo on her wrist described her self-image—*Born Loser!* She was ready to quit. On several occasions that week, Jerry spent time with Venus—on the basketball court and in the dining room. He reminded her of God's great love for her, of God's plans for her life. And he told her that Bible college was exactly where she should be. In fact, he threatened her, "You'd better be here when I come back to visit this school. If you're not, I'm going to have to go looking for you."

Venus stayed at Bible school that year and then returned for another year. And she grew in her faith in the Lord.

Recently, she came for a visit on her way to a special Christian native conference in southern Alberta. It was the first time the conference had invited specific native women; and she had been chosen to attend from New Brunswick, where she had been working with Northern Canada Evangelical Mission® for many years. While here with us, she asked Jerry to drive her back downtown in Calgary. She pointed out the spots: "I got thrown out of that bar. I used to sleep over there." And then she gave us a book that was recently published, *"Keepers of the Faith,"* containing the stories of five native women. Each story was an amazing example of God's power to change people's lives when they allow God to work. Venus was one of them. What a testament to a big God!

God is perfectly capable of arranging the right contact at the right time. Whenever it happens, it reminds us again that our God really is big enough!

There was the time when Jerry was attending a conference at Prairie Bible Institute in Three Hills and was hoping to meet up with Matt. He had chatted with Matt on a previous occasion and felt that he needed to follow up with him. The only problem was that Matt was nowhere to be seen. All weekend Jerry looked for him. After three days, Jerry prayed, "God, you are going to have to bring him to me."

Just before leaving the area after the conference, Jerry wanted to check out an oil problem on his car that was parked about two blocks away from the college. He was in the process when he heard someone call, "Hey, do you need some help? I used to be a heavy duty mechanic." And, sure enough, there was Matt! With five minutes to spare, Jerry was able to connect Matt with another mission representative that was looking for people with Matt's background.

Then there were two previous contacts at Briercrest Bible College that Jerry was hoping to find. He had talked with these two individuals the last time he was there, but there was one problem in trying to track them down again. He did not even know their names! Again he prayed, "Dear God, if you want me to connect with them, please bring them across my path." That night after dinner, Jerry was just heading out the dining room door as someone was coming in. Sure enough, it was one of the individuals he had wanted to see. Later that night, Jerry had some spare time and went up to the library to use a computer. When he was finished, he couldn't get out of the library again. The door he had used to get in was now locked. He headed down the library counter looking for someone to ask for help. A person was standing down the way with his back towards Jerry—and you guessed it—when the fellow turned around, there was the second person Jerry had wanted to see. God knew exactly where they were and how to make the connection!

Jerry was in a hurry, heading home after being up at Peace River Bible Institute in northwestern Alberta. While there had been some good contacts with students, there really was not anything significant to report to GOM about potential prospects for them. As Jerry was sailing past Drayton Valley, he thought about Vikki, a teacher there in the Christian school. Vikki had come from a difficult home situation, mostly raised by grandparents. It was through the influence of Camp Little Red that she really found the Lord. She had also been discipled doing many of the Bible correspondence lessons in the David & Jonathan program. It had been wonderful to see her progressing, becoming a camp counselor, going to Peace River Bible College, getting her teaching degree at university, and even going back to camp as a speaker one week. Jerry considered stopping in to see if he could find Vikki, but he didn't know where to look, and he was in a hurry! Besides, Vikki would be in the middle of class. So, Jerry kept going.

He was almost out of town when that voice came to him, *"Go back and find Vikki."*

"But I don't even know what school she teaches in," Jerry protested. But he knew he had better obey.

He turned back into the town and the first school he came to, he stopped to check at the office. "Do you have a teacher here named Vikki Waisman?" he inquired.

"Yes," the receptionist said. "She's our Grade 2 teacher."

"Well, I know she'll be in class right now, but maybe I could just write a message and leave it for her. I'm just on my way through to Calgary," said Jerry.

"Oh, I'll just page her for you," said the receptionist. And she immediately began to call over the intercom, "Vikki Waisman, Vikki Waisman, can you come to the office please?"

Vikki was delighted to see Jerry and invited him to come and visit her class. The students were in the middle of writing a test, but she told them to put their pencils down as she had a guest she wanted them to meet. Jerry talked to the children a few minutes, telling them what he did. Then he prepared to leave. Vikki walked him out of the classroom and then said, "I'm so glad you came by today. I think God must have sent you. I've really been thinking that I'd like to go to South America doing some sort of missions, but I don't know what to do or how to get there. Could you help get me going?"

It was definitely a God appointment. Vikki began communicating with Len Lane from GOM and within the year she was on her way to Peru. We were reminded that we just need to be faithful, obeying what God tells us to do. He can bring the right contacts at the right time. He is a big God!

Each day brings fresh opportunities. Each day, whether we're involved in specific mentoring situations, organized ministry opportunities, or mobilizing for missions around the world; or whether we are changing the oil in our vehicle, or doing laundry, it is a constant challenge to live life with God's priorities. What an encouragement to receive this email from a student at Briercrest:

> Thanks so much for the e-mail! You're really a blessing to me. And my sister appreciated the words you had for her too—it was great that she got the chance to meet you. If you could continue praying that I would be sensitive to hear God's direction and submissive to respond to it, that would be awesome. I really want to get going on the opportunities that are available to me—the

last thing I want is to ignore His call and end up living the "American dream."

I really appreciate your prayers for me, Jerry. You've shown me a welcoming love that I too seldom see in the missionaries I encounter; it's very encouraging and inspiring. Hopefully I'll see you again before He comes!

Matthew

16

THE COSTA RICA CONNECTION

Beginnings in 1997

It's all my mother's fault—she's the one that died and started the ball rolling.

Now there are two things that need explaining about that comment. First is the blame game! It began years ago when our children were quite young. We took them for a rare treat to a nearby McDonald's restaurant. As we sat eating our food, we suddenly became focused on the family dynamics at the table next to us. A mother and a small boy were struggling with setting their order of items on the table. The boy was not cooperating, and was being quite vocal with his protests. Our children were not impressed with the behavior—the mother was angrily berating the boy with some colorful language, and the boy was talking right back to her. In the commotion, the boy knocked over a tall chocolate milk shake, and it spilled all over the table and floor. Now the mother was really upset, haranguing her son for being so careless. And the boy? He shot right back, "It's all your fault—you're the one that bought the dumb drink!"

Needless to say, our children were shocked at such rude conduct. They all had visions of what would have happened to them if they had tried that kind of back talk to their parents! In fact, it made such an impression on them, that it became a family saying that stuck over the years. It worked in all kinds of situations. If Jeremy was teasing his sisters, one of the girls would attack me with the blame game: "It's all your fault—you're the one that had the dumb boy!" If one of our sons-in-law was protesting about something his wife wanted to do, I would happily remind him, "It's all your fault—you're the one that married the dumb girl!"

So, it is perfectly logical to blame the Costa Rica connection on Mom Cornell, especially in light of the second thing that needs explaining. Mom had not really planned on dying when she did. I guess that could be said for most of us! However, she had been hoping to go once more and visit my sister, Marilyn Longworth, and her family who are missionaries in Costa Rica. They had built an addition onto their house, and Mom really would have liked to see it. While Mom had been to Costa Rica three or four times over the years, Jerry and I had only been once before at Christmas time in 1980 when Marilyn had gotten married. We had to go then to make sure it was really happening, since Marilyn was in her mid-30s!

When Mom passed away, we got to thinking that perhaps one of the best things we could do with funds she had left behind was to take our whole family to Costa Rica and visit the

Longworths in the summer of 1997. One night that spring, we thought our kids were asleep upstairs, but they all suddenly appeared when they overheard us talking about the wild possibility of visiting Costa Rica. They were incredulous at the thought. They could not believe it! Neither could we! We would never have considered making an expensive trip like that with a family of six—if it hadn't been for Mom. And so, like I said, it was all Mom's fault!

When the big day came, we were all so excited. Our flights were with American Airlines going through Dallas, TX; then over to Miami, FL; and finally on to San Jose, Costa Rica. In Dallas, there was a delay because of mechanical difficulties. By the time we got to Miami, our planeload of people was being added to another; and, as a result, it was over-booked. We began to hear announcements calling for passengers willing to take a bump. They were offering $300 per passenger in travel vouchers for anyone willing to give up his or her seat for a later flight. We were not willing. We had four children who were so excited to get to Costa Rica. A delay? Forget it! But Jerry was listening—and by now the offer had gone up to $500. Then it was $700.

When it reached $1,000, Jerry pushed us all to the counter. The ticket agent asked, "How many in your party?"

We said, "Six."

"That's exactly the number of seats we need to find yet," she said.

So, the airline rebooked us for the next morning, gave us all travel vouchers for $1,000 US (more than the cost of our original tickets), handed us meal vouchers for supper and breakfast, and provided us with two rooms in a motel. We called the Longworths to advise them of the delay, and headed off to a great supper. We couldn't even spend the full value of the meal vouchers. It was too much food!

With the travel vouchers we received that time, our whole family was able to go back to Costa Rica again in 1998. And guess what. We got bumped again—this time for $500 travel vouchers! So we went a third time. After three trips to Costa Rica, we had acquired enough travel points on the American Airline award program that we got a fourth trip free as well. Mom's money went a long ways! A big God indeed!

Those Costa Rican trips were a wonderful provision from God to allow our children to visit a mission field and to get to know their Costa Rican cousins. There were other bonuses along the way as well. A Costa Rican friend of the Longworths made a twelve-passenger van available to us for the time we were there. With our family, and the Longworths' five, we even had one seat to spare! Also, a Calgary supporter had a time-share in a resort motel on the Pacific side of Costa Rica. The units were two-bedroom apartments with kitchenettes. What a special highlight to be able to spend a week of refreshment, together with the Longworths, so economically!

But the sights and sounds of Costa Rica made an impression. There were such contrasts—luxury homes right across from tin and black-tarpaper shacks. It was a religious nation, but it was so sad to see people crawling on their knees long distances, hoping to earn favor with God. Down town San Jose was overwhelming with push cart vendors, so many people, smells, vehicles honking, and narrow streets. It was a beautiful country, yet there was garbage everywhere. There was breath-taking flowering shrubbery, but with bars on every window and door it looked more like a prison camp. Short distances took long traveling times with traffic jams and windy, pothole roads.

That first trip to Costa Rica, we spent a day visiting with Dorothy Rempel who lived right in San Jose. She was the lady that had worked in CEF of Saskatchewan right before Jerry arrived there. Dorothy was an exceptional missionary, and in spite of being a little older than us, she did not seem to know it. She wanted our kids to go on a *paseo* (an outing) to a park over-looking a valley and play home-free-hide-and-go-seek. She was unbelievable—hiding herself by plopping down at a picnic table with a family of total strangers, borrowing one of their children's hats, and pretending she was part of their group. The family just loved it, and so did our kids.

But while up on that hill, as the sun began to disappear, we looked down over the Orosi valley and saw hundreds of little lights. It was a beautiful sight; but, as Dorothy informed us, it was a very needy valley. Very little gospel outreach was happening there. For some reason, Jerry was deeply moved. We prayed together, and wondered about all those homes in that valley. Who would reach them with the gospel?

It was September of 2003. We were again in Costa Rica, visiting my sister and her family. Since our Spanish was non-existent, we spent most of our time doing maintenance projects for them. While we were there, Jerry sensed that God was speaking to him about being open for something new. Night after night, it seemed like God would wake Jerry up and challenge him about the needs around him in Costa Rica. One night, he woke me up and said, "I think God might be calling us to Costa Rica."

I laughed, thinking about Jerry's hopeless language skills, and said, "Tell me about it in the morning."

The next morning, Jerry began to share what he felt God was showing him. It sounded interesting, but rather impractical. We were still responsible for the David & Jonathan Inc. ministry back in Alberta, we still had children at home, and Jerry's folks were needing more help. We prayed about it and went down for breakfast.

At the table that morning, my sister announced that we were going to go on a *paseo* to visit some friends. They had to deliver something to these friends and thought it would make a nice picnic destination. The man, Juan, used to serve with his wife as one of the house parent couples at the children's home where Marilyn had worked for many years. After his wife died, Juan had remarried Esther, an American lady who had worked as a professor in Costa Rica. Esther had poured her life savings into setting up a retreat center on five acres of prime land in the Orosi valley, that same valley we had prayed over years before.

When we arrived on the property, it was beautiful—all the fruit trees, so many exotic birds and flowers. Jerry sensed a tug in his spirit, *"This is the place I've been talking to you about."*

As a means of contact with the local people, Esther had been offering English and computer classes, as well as soccer and swimming opportunities. She had been trying to gradually add to the facilities so the property could be used for church retreats and outreach. Because of their age and deteriorating health, Esther and Juan needed to turn the property over to someone else to run. But to whom? Then she asked us what we had done in life. As Jerry began to tell her of our background in children's ministries and camping, Esther's eyes got bigger and bigger.

She said, "I believe you are the couple God wants to take over this property." They were willing to sell it to us for the $80,000. US they had originally paid in spite of the extra value in all the improvements that had been made.

Wow! God moved on our hearts to pay attention. Did He have a part for us? We agreed to pray about it. For the next few days, we talked about the possibilities and potential with the Longworths. Esther had promised to be in touch, as she had to work things out with another party in the States who had defaulted on his earlier agreement with Esther to buy the place for a ministry center.

Two days before leaving Costa Rica, we talked again with Esther and SLAM! God had shut the door. The other party wanted to keep it after all. And that was the end of it—or so we thought. But why would God have seemingly set everything in place just to have it all fall apart? We were confused about what God was doing. Had we misunderstood His promptings?

A year and a half later, in January 2005, Jerry kept waking up at night, thinking about Esther's property in Costa Rica. It was as if the Lord was telling him to get in touch with Esther about that property. We decided to send a casual New Year's greeting by email. Almost immediately, we got a response. The former purchaser was still in default, but had now issued threats about getting his down payment back. Even though his investment on the property purchase had been from monies receipted in the States as charitable donations, he wanted it all back to refurbish a private theatre, and he was threatening legal action. Esther and Juan had already reinvested the down payment funds into improvements on the property, so they had no money to pay him what he was demanding. They did not know what to do. With all the stress and turmoil, Esther had suffered a serious stroke, and her husband, Juan, was having heart issues. They were desperate, and still wanted us to consider taking over the property.

When we had first thought about trying to take on the project ourselves, we knew it would be a huge job. We would need to set it up as a charitable organization for receipting in Canada and the USA, have a board of directors assembled to satisfy Costa Rican law as well as Canadian and US requirements, have all the bylaws and policies drafted, have Spanish speaking personnel to operate it, have funds raised to pay the expenses, and so on. But again we prayed, "Yes, Lord, if this is from You, we are willing." We figured we would use our retirement savings and try to get others to invest in the project as well. In our minds, the one critical hurdle was finding key Spanish-speaking people who would live on site to manage the property and develop ministry. We agreed with Esther that we would wait upon the Lord until May to see how He would provide for personnel. We knew that was a small matter for God if He really wanted us to move ahead with the project. We began making phone calls and sending emails. But as the weeks and months passed, and we still had no Spanish personnel in sight, we were no longer so sure. In fact, we were more and more confused. Was this really of God? Why was there no one willing to help? After exhausting all our contacts, we finally decided that we would have to tell Esther we just did not have the human resources to take it on. It was very difficult to contact Esther and release that opportunity that day. Why did the Lord keep bringing that property back into our lives?

Later that same day, the phone rang. It was Len Lane from Global Outreach Mission. We were still working with David & Jonathan Inc. and we hadn't been in touch with Len for some time. He was just calling to let us know that he planned to come from Ontario to Alberta for a special celebration weekend with Venture Teams International. He wondered if we might be planning on attending it as well. During the course of the conversation, he asked if we had heard from Costa Rica lately. Len had a special interest in Costa Rica because, when he had previously been in Calgary working with VTI, several short-term missions' teams had been sent to Costa Rica using the Longworths as their contact. At first, Jerry did not want to talk about Costa Rica. He was still upset and confused over not being able to move ahead with that property. But throughout their phone call, Len kept bringing up the topic. Finally, Jerry began to share about the property we had been offered…and Len got excited! He explained that GOM had been looking for a base to service their Central American missionaries. They wanted it for dental and medical teams plus other short-term ministry teams. Maybe this property was just what they were looking for! Len asked about getting together with Jerry for coffee the coming weekend to find out more.

After Len saw our pictures of the property that weekend, he could hardly wait to get back and talk with the president of GOM. Monday morning, Jerry emailed Esther about this new possibility. But SLAM! The door got shut again! Esther replied that right after we had turned it down, a Costa Rican church group arrived to look at the property to use for conference grounds. They planned to purchase it, so it was conditionally sold. She said she was so sorry, but it was gone. We could not believe it. Why had God kept this property on our hearts for so long, only to allow it to be snatched away again, for a second time?

A few days later, Esther emailed again. She said, "You'll never believe this, but even though that Costa Rican church was planning to buy the property, the church leaders changed their minds. When they were on their way to the bank to get the money, they got talking about it among themselves and decided that it was not going to be a big enough land area for their vision. So, it is back on the table."

In June, Jerry ended up flying down to Buffalo, NY to meet with the president of GOM and to share the story about that property. Next, the president and two others flew down to Costa Rica to meet Esther and check out the property for themselves. They liked what they saw, and drew up a purchase agreement. The transfer was to happen that September.

We were excited, and Global Outreach Mission was excited! Then we got a phone call from Len Lane. Apparently there was a little hitch. Esther & Juan needed some purchase money up front so they could relocate off the property. But GOM had hoped they could pay Esther off gradually. The mission did not have any extra funds to use for a substantial down payment. Jerry said we would really pray about it.

A couple nights later, in the middle of the night, Jerry again could not sleep. It seemed there was a little discussion going on between him and the Lord. It was as if the Lord was saying, *"Jerry, you were willing to use your savings to buy the property once, why not now?"*

"Well," argued Jerry, *"there's just one problem, Lord. Before, it was me that was going to own it."*

"Does it really matter who owns it?" said that quiet voice.

The next morning after Jerry talked it over with me, we both felt we needed to call GOM and break our "alabaster box" before the Lord. Jerry told Len, "We will give the $100,000 CN (which was the equivalent of $80,000 US at that time) for the full purchase price of the property."

Len thanked us and said he would get back to us. In just a couple days, the board members of GOM said they had discussed our proposal, but they did not feel right about depleting our retirement savings to that extent at this stage of our lives. They would accept only $50,000 CN; but it was to be on a loan basis, and they would seek to return $10,000 each year. That amount would give Esther the initial funds needed to relocate, and she was willing for them to pay her the remainder over time. That day, I think we felt a little like Abraham must have felt, offering up Isaac. Just as God had arranged a *"ram in the thicket"* in place of Isaac, so He had arranged for our own *"ram in the thicket"*—a plan whereby our offered retirement savings would come back to us over a period of years.

Then a few more days passed, and Len called again. He said, "You won't believe this, but our president was down in Texas telling the crazy story of this Costa Rica property, and a man gave GOM $50,000 towards the project. That was just the amount needed, along with our funds, to purchase the property in full! Wow! How big is your God! Is He big enough?

In January 2006, the first missions' trip was heading to Costa Rica; and Jerry had been urged to go along because of his part in securing the Orosi property. Not only had we learned lessons about God's timing, but we also began to realize that God was way ahead of us in managing all the details. There were so many needs to take care of and so many areas to develop for the Costa Rican project. How wonderful that God had placed the property into the hands of a well-established mission with the practical and human resources, as well as the experience required to give oversight. And it was wonderful to see things progressing.

That first team tore down a *rancho* (like a picnic area with a tin roof for shelter) and began the initial work for a multi-purpose building 42' x 70'. Forty-five holes had to be dug by hand around the perimeter, and the workers only had short-handled shovels to use! It was tough work in rocky ground, and no one was too impressed when it was discovered that the measurements on one side were out by several inches and all the holes had to be redone. What a job! Finally the walls were erected. Then other work teams went down and the roof went on. Later, a team of engineers and other professionals from the United States volunteered its expertise to do a ten-year development plan for the property. What great fellowship the various teams of volunteers had as they caught the vision of the potential for that property. Missionary personnel expressed interest in moving down and managing it. Others arrived to begin church services there. Esther and Juan were thrilled at what was happening.

Then we got word that our supporting church in Abbotsford was interested in sending a team down with us to help in January 2007. What a special encouragement! What a scary proposition for us to head up this team! Jerry and I were both excited as we began to plan the details.

17

THE DREAM TEAM

January 2008

A t last it was to be our turn! Grace Evangelical Bible Church in Abbotsford, BC had a history of sending teams to do projects for the missionaries they helped to support. It was a great way for the church people to catch a glimpse of the needs and outreaches they supported around the world and to see their missionaries in action. Teams had traveled to China and to the Ukraine, but somehow, traveling over the provincial border to Calgary, where we live, just did not have quite the same appeal. Then Grace Church learned about the Costa Rican project.

The fall of 2007, Jerry began talking with Verne, a king pin in initiating the missions' trips from Abbotsford. There was a good group interested-a—about 13 in all—in heading to Costa

Rica right after New Year's. There were mission applications to complete plus travel and food costs to be collected for the team, besides raising funds to cover the work projects. While there were a number of projects that needed doing at the Costa Rican property, the main project we were hoping to take on was the building of a four-plex cabin including washrooms. The cabin would have four separate bedrooms to accommodate two or three bunk beds, each bedroom having an outside entrance and inside access to the washroom facilities in the cabin. The additional sleeping capacity would be a big asset for groups using the facilities.

While Jerry and I had directed various ministries and had done lots of children's outreach and teacher training, we had never been responsible for an overseas mission team. We felt a little out of our element with all the customs issues, lining up projects in another country, navigating in a foreign language, and so on. The team members were experts in their fields, and we wanted the trip to be worthwhile for them. We did our best to get all the arrangements in place ahead of time.

But, sure enough, the trouble started. Satan was doing his best to thwart the trip even before it began. First off, there was a staffing crisis in Costa Rica. The on-site project manager was asked to leave. Then the camp managers resigned and were gone by the end of November. The couple that was working with the church plant on the property was having serious issues, both physically and personally. That left nobody in charge down there! Who would make all the arrangements on site for our January work team? Who would get building supplies lined up? Who would be there to translate for the team? But in spite of the turmoil, God had it all under control. God arranged for a special missionary couple to be reassigned temporarily from elsewhere in Costa Rica in order to be on site three weeks ahead to facilitate our team.

Next, the property was red-ticketed. That meant our proposed project of building a cabin was on hold until building permit issues were resolved. So what were top-notch workers going to do with plane tickets already purchased? Larry, one of the team members, who was an exceptional building contractor, kept asking Verne what the project was going to be. Verne kept putting him off. Jerry talked with Verne, and Verne talked with Jerry. Finally, in spite of the project obstacles and uncertainties, Verne said, "I think we should go and trust the Lord."

Jerry said, "I agree. If there is no project, at least we can have a great time on the beach." There was no nearby beach, but that was beside the point.

Then attacks began on the team members: one got shingles, another broke her wrist, two got severe cases of flu. Some even considered canceling out with the health concerns. In the end, everyone decided to go.

There was one more problem—the weather. January is supposed to be dry season in Costa Rica, but just prior to our arrival it had rained for forty-four days straight. Several houses on the opposite riverbank adjacent to the property were tipping precariously over the edge as the swollen river had washed out the ground underneath. How were we going to be able to do outside construction projects if it kept raining?

Finally, on Friday, January 4, the team arrived in Costa Rica. It was about 10:00 p.m. by the time the last ones cleared customs and we all met outside the airport terminal. Everything was different: temperature, dress, vegetation, smells, currency, language. Thankfully, my sister and brother-in-law, Marilyn and Dave Longworth, had come to greet us, so we had some Spanish interpreters. Two of the ladies from Abbotsford were retired missionaries from Spanish-speaking countries so they were able to help with translation as well. We all crammed our luggage in the back sections of a little bus and climbed aboard for the 1 ½ hour trip down to the property. It was after midnight when we arrived, so we quickly found our bunks—no queen-sized beds!—and settled in.

Ouch! OUCH! The bunks were built for kids and did not have much headroom! It only took a time or two of clunking your head to remember to duck when you crawled out of bed in the morning. Local ladies did the cooking and put out wonderful meals in spite of limited facilities. After breakfast, it was time for devotions and team orientation. By this time, the word had leaked out to all of the team members—we were not sure what our project would be—or if we would even have one! We prayed.

We walked around the camp and noted minor maintenance jobs that could be taken care of, and again we prayed. We looked across the river at the houses tipping over the embankment, and we prayed about the weather. Then we walked and swayed across the very long suspended footbridge at the end of our property and did a little tour of the nearby town of Orosi. We saw people, needy people, and we prayed. That evening we all retired early. We were still catching up on sleep and getting ready for what we hoped would be a busy two weeks.

Sunday morning, we all attended the service that was being held in the multi-purpose building on the property. It was a unique experience to catch the atmosphere of our Christian brothers and sisters there. Part of the service was interpreted, so it was nice to be able to understand some things. Esther and Juan were there, too, and we were delighted to reconnect with them.

After lunch, the government official arrived to meet with the men. He had been part of the planning committee for the government in upgrading building codes and regulations for Costa Rica. It was within his power to grant—or not to grant—permission to proceed with a project. He did not speak English, so everything was done through an interpreter. He began by asking each man his name and what job he had done. Larry started. He owned a construction company and was a building contractor for many years with several crews working for him in the Fraser Valley. The government man said Costa Rica had special codes for earthquake zones. "Oh, we understand that," said Larry. "We have earthquakes in BC, and we have very strict building codes there."

Next was Verne. He owned and operated a crane company and was an expert welder. Norm was a draftsman and had his own business. Pete and Bill Lessley were both carpenters with many years' experience. Walter was a roof inspector. Craig was only nineteen, but had also done a lot of building. In fact, he did the fancy spiral staircases for Larry. But he told the government official he had really come to Costa Rica to find a wife. And then he asked the man if he had any daughters. We were all shocked at his audacity. The government man must have wondered if he had heard correctly and asked, through the interpreter, for Craig to repeat what he had said. Craig did, and then began to laugh—a deep infectious laugh. Then the government man began to laugh. The ice was broken! And the government man said, "Yes, I do. And I'll bring her around on Wednesday."

Then there was Bill Cornwall. He sat with his face away from the group, staring at the wall. When he was asked why he came, he said, "I don't know why I'm here except my wife made me come." Bill had been a mechanic for many years, but was also a landscaper. He felt totally inadequate with all the expertise of the construction people.

After hearing from everyone, the government man thought for a minute. "Well," he said, "I will give you permission to do the kitchen project—replacing the entire roof, revamping the interior, and so on. And you can do the bars on the windows and doors of the multi-purpose building. I'll be back to inspect your work." Although it was not what we expected, we had a project. Thank you, Lord!

But now we needed to quickly assemble the needed supplies. The little Toyota truck was very busy hauling lumber—until it broke down. But whom did we have along with us? Bill, the mechanic! He stuck his head under the hood and investigated. It needed a clutch cylinder but the part might not be available for four to six weeks. So Bill set to work improvising, and in no time he had the truck serviced and running. God had brought Bill for a purpose after all!

Meanwhile, the men began removing the kitchen roof. We prayed again about the rain. For 9 ½ days God held off the rain. Every morning we were up early for breakfast. The men took turns leading a group devotional. And then it was off to work by about 7:30 a.m. All day we worked till it got dark—around 6:30 p.m. The couple filling in to manage the camp could hardly keep our crew supplied with building materials. They began calling us "The Dream Team." In all their years of hosting missions' teams, they said they had never had such a capable team that worked so hard and got along so well together.

While some were dismantling the kitchen roof, the carpenters were building a temporary counter and cupboard for the cooks to use in another building. How would you like the responsibility of cooking three meals a day for about twenty-five people when your kitchen is torn apart! The national cooks were amazing.

Two of the ladies from Abbotsford "just happened" to have experience in designing commercial kitchens. They set to work drafting the interior options, deciding what equipment was needed, and then going shopping for new cupboards and appliances. Others got busy with painting, cleaning, sewing, and sorting resource supplies. The two retired Spanish-speaking missionaries both had nursing backgrounds, so they did medical out-trips. Another lady organized a children's program on site.

And then there was Bill. When he finished repairing the truck, Bill discovered a shed full of weed eaters and other lawn equipment that needed fixing and overhauling, so he got busy doing that. When he looked around the grounds, he saw that there was more pruning and landscaping to be done than he would ever have time to finish. And so, besides pestering the cooks, Bill was having the time of his life getting acquainted with and caring for all the fruit trees, shrubbery, and wild flowers on the property.

But it was not all work. One day we headed out in a rented bus to visit a national park. The team members were anticipating going on a zip-line ride through the rain forest when, suddenly, strange noises started coming from the bus's internal workings.

Apparently an accelerator cable pin had fallen off, and the gears kept revving. Thankfully, it happened right by a scenic pull-off, so most of us enjoyed stretching our legs and wandering around a bit. The Spanish-speaking driver was scrambling to work out how to get his passengers to their destination. He left the bus and headed off to a place ahead to try to make other arrangements for us. Meanwhile, we had Bill. And we had Verne and a few other handymen. They lifted up the floor of the bus to take a look down under. After sizing up the problem, Bill said, "I think we need a number "something-or-other" bolt. There should be one on this bus somewhere." And sure enough, they found one—on the back bumper—just the perfect size! They almost had the bus all back together when the bus driver returned with alternate transportation. You can imagine what must have been going on in his mind to see his bus undergoing unauthorized surgery! What a blessing to have Bill along, the guy who didn't know why he came! And the team got to enjoy the zipline excursion after all!

Bill even found something to do the afternoon we visited a very poor area of San Jose that was nicknamed "The Pit." Generations of refugees live in shanty housing in a bowl-shaped narrow valley. Since they do not have citizenship, they can't get accreditation for school, nor can they work legally. The living conditions were shocking. We had brought along several suitcases of children's clothing as well as some candy treats and small toys for the children. Of course most of us could only smile and gesture to communicate. But the grins of appreciation spoke clearly. We began climbing our way up the steep embankments after all the clothes were distributed, and then Jerry and Bill saw a young man walking towards them. They offered him a treat and his face lit up with a toothless grin. As Jerry and Bill continued up the path, suddenly Bill stopped. He said to Jerry, "Wait, I've got to do something." Quickly he went back to catch up with the young man. Bill pulled off his own new Chicago baseball hat and plunked it on the man's head. Again the man smiled, and then started to reach up to return the hat. Bill shook his head and gestured that it was for the man. The smile got even bigger. And when Bill got back to where Jerry was waiting, he said, "That's one for the Lord." Of course when Bill arrived back at the retreat property, he had to find himself a new hat in the dress-up clothes. For the rest of the time, he wore a blue straw "up-side-down-plant-pot-look-a-like" hat—that is, except for the times he tried to plant it on one of the cooks' heads!

By the end of the two weeks, it was perfectly obvious to all of us why God had arranged for our team to do the kitchen project. We had the perfect people there for just that job! How amazing to have that caliber of workmen assembled with exactly the right skills. Even the pump in the swimming pool was repaired for under five dollars instead of requiring a costly motor replacement. And on the last afternoon, after holding off for all our construction on the roof, the rain began to fall. How big is your God?

Our team also did some work on a five-bedroom typical Costa Rican home right across the road from the property. It had been on the market for sale for some time, but since it was not selling readily, GOM had arranged a lease agreement with the owner so they could house the new property manager family that would be arriving from the States that spring. GOM did not have the resources in place to purchase the house right then; but, as part of the lease agreement, it was determined that, if an offer came in, GOM would have 48 hours to match it.

A couple months after getting back home, we got news on a Friday afternoon: someone had made an offer on the house for $25,000. Unless GOM matched it within 48 hours, it would be sold just before the new family was to arrive in Costa Rica. The GOM offices were already closed for the weekend out in Ontario and New York, and we had no way of knowing if they had heard of the situation. We tried phoning Len Lane at home, but with no success. We stood looking at each other and wondered what could be done. Jerry said, "You know we have to buy it somehow, don't you!" I agreed.

At that moment, a solution popped into our heads. "Why don't we tell Global to charge our support account with a debit for that amount? Then we will just have to trust God to provide the funds to cover the debit." When we finally got hold of GOM board members with our suggestion, they agreed it was a good option as the housing was urgently needed and they did not have general fund reserves to designate for that project. So, by the deadline, GOM was able to match the offer.

Within a week, we had a call from a man in Edmonton. "We want to make a donation towards that Costa Rican house project—$9,000. And that was just the start. We could hardly keep up with writing thank you notes to donors for the project. By that summer, Jerry got an email from our head office that over $20,000 had already come in. The tears began rolling down his cheeks. Within just a few more months, all the funds were in. Again, God had overwhelmed us with His supply! What a big God!

18

All These Things Shall be Added

Housing and Vehicles

Housing

After our experience in 1974 with trying to get into the housing market in Abbotsford, we figured home ownership was beyond us with our very modest level of salary. When we moved back to Alberta, we were happily housed in the one bedroom basement suite of our Bible school president. We had carved out a portion of the large living room for our office. It was cozy, but adequate. Then Jeremy arrived in 1979.

My Dad began to talk to us about our housing situation. Some years earlier, he and Mom had scraped together their meager resources along with two more mortgages to invest in a rental home—an up and down duplex. It was their way of trying to provide some retirement income for the future since Dad had no retirement pension plan benefit through the Bible college where he worked. The rental place had been both a blessing and a curse. It really was a financial blessing, but the maintenance work involved in the rental property was sometimes overwhelming. Besides having wood siding, the house had 23 exterior windows plus their storm windows, each with wooden frames that required painting. Then there was all the interior maintenance of the suites. No matter how well Dad tried to screen renters, there were often some nasty surprises left behind when the renters moved out.

By 1979, Dad & Mom still had a few years remaining to pay off their mortgage; but Dad said he and Mom had talked it over and wanted to offer us a deal. They had the place appraised at about $65,000 but they said they would sell it to us for $55,000 and personally hold the mortgage for us at 8%. That sounded wonderful to us since at that time, rates were much higher. Even Canada Savings Bonds were yielding 19% interest in those years. There were more great terms available to us. We could put down whatever we wanted, and choose our own monthly payment amount. How can you beat that? But we were still apprehensive. Home ownership seemed like a huge commitment for us.

We finally decided to accept the offer. The seller, Dad, even helped us repaint the walls and kitchen cupboards, and gave us a hand in the move. What a blessing! So when Jeremy was about three months old, God provided us with our own home. Our payments were $450 per month, but we were able to rent the basement suite for $325. In the 12 ½ years it took us to pay off our mortgage, we only paid $125 out of pocket each month for our housing. And for most of those years, Jerry's younger sister, Shirley, rented our suite—a very convenient babysitter!

By the time we had finished paying for the house, Jeremy was ready for Junior High and would have to change schools since his school only included elementary classes. Another campus of the same Christian school that our children attended was located in the northeast quadrant of the city. It went all the way from kindergarten through Grade 12, so we would have the option of sending all our children to one location instead of having to shuttle between two schools. At the same time, we were facing accommodation dilemmas in our first home. With three girls sharing one bedroom, we wondered if we should take over the rental suite downstairs for an office and extra bedroom. Or should we just relocate? Our neighborhood was becoming less attractive with many places turning into rentals. We decided we would do some looking at homes over in the northeast close to the main school campus just to see what was out there.

Our realtor called us, one day, to view a four-level split home in the estate area of Castleridge. Immediately we protested. We were not "estate" type people. We were missionaries. However, the realtor assured us that this area was not overly pricey. Besides being in a flight path, it was an ethnic community, and those factors affected the market value. It didn't bother us! We were missionaries. People of all backgrounds are important to God! We were mostly concerned with space and convenient location, not prestige! Besides, what an opportunity for our children to glimpse a "world" view in our own neighborhood.

The place did seem ideal for our needs, but in our minds there was a big gap price-wise between the two homes. The realtor did a quick estimate on ours, and we were amazed. In the 12 ½ years we had owned it, our house had over doubled in value, and it was very close to the asking price of the estate home. Since the housing market was tight that year, we knew we had to act quickly if we wanted to make an offer on the estate home. Sure enough, two other offers came in at the same time. We put forward our best offer unconditionally. And we got it!

There was one problem. Our home wasn't even listed yet. We did not get much sleep that night. What had we done? It was a possibility to keep our home as a rental property, but the maintenance would be time consuming—time we did not have. Besides, banks were not too eager about extending mortgages to people at our income level! That weekend, the realtor ran an impromptu open house. There were eight parties that came to see the house that afternoon, and five of them were neighbors. Amazingly, by day's end, we had three offers to purchase! What a big God!

There were a couple things we needed for the new place. The former owners were taking their fridge, so that was one item. And our couch set, after 22 years, was falling apart. Again, just at the right moment, Jerry's grandmother decided to give her grandchildren another $1,000 legacy. We found a good quality second-hand couch, loveseat and chair for $600 and a scratch-and-dent new fridge for $400. The dent happened to be on the side that would sit right up against the counter! Thank you God!

The realtor, at his own cost, had even made arrangements for a professional mover to move us. Apparently, as part of his real estate service for his clients, the realtor had a long-standing agreement to pay the moving company $500 a move. What a lesson the movers learned when they agreed to move us! Never again would they sign a moving contract for $500, sight unseen. When the moving van arrived early on moving day, the men walked in and looked around. We had everything packed and ready to load. We had even already filled our own vehicles with all our closet clothes, plants and lampshades. But they were stunned at the amount yet to move. It was actually like moving two complete households, since Jerry's sister was moving with us temporarily until she found her own place. We also had our piano, all our office equipment—desks, filing cabinets, books, etc. Out in the garage, besides the usual workshop tools and garden equipment, there was also a set of wooden sunroom furniture that Mom had bought for us for the new place. As the movers walked through the house, they kept saying, "Holy #$%@!" They immediately got on the phone to their company and ordered two additional moving vans complete with extra crews. It was late afternoon before the first of the moving vans finally arrived at our new place.

The next morning in our new home, we got up and looked around. We couldn't believe it was ours. But then it wasn't. It was really God's! He was just allowing us to enjoy this place for a time. Everything was so practical for our needs. We even discovered special features we had not observed on our walk-through. How good God was to us! Because of how God had worked out all the details, we had no house payments. The money we would have normally budgeted from our income for housing could go instead towards Christian schooling for our children.

VEHICLES

While acquiring and maintaining a vehicle was not in the same league as purchasing a home, it was another area in which we often saw God provide. Back in the early '70s, we didn't even own the car we were driving, since CEF of Saskatchewan provided the vehicle. But the tires were wearing out and we had been praying for tires—new tires! A couple that taught clubs for us out at the Bible school in Pambrun was also praying for tires. With several small children, they were living on a shoestring budget while attending classes. Sometimes we prayed together with them about our mutual needs. One day, Henry Friesen had been walking home from school, praying about meat for his family. Just then a partridge hit the wire overhead and fell dead at his feet. This time, the need was tires!

Then someone gave us some good used tires. We were delighted. But then a thought occurred to us. Was this God's answer for us? Or for the Friesen family? We really did not know. We thought the tires would be wonderful for us, but we were reminded that we had been praying for new tires. We finally decided to give them away to the Friesens. And within the week, a man from a dealership called us to come get some new tires on our vehicle. How big is your God?

Two times God switched vehicles for us. Once was when we had purchased a '68 Ford on the advice of a mechanic uncle. It turned out to have many "issues," along with its 100,000 miles. We really needed a vehicle that would pull a travel trailer, but this was not the car we had hoped it would be. What should we do now? We were out in BC en route to the coast and stopped overnight at Jerry's grandparents, then living in Kelowna. Out of the clear blue, his grandpa said he wanted to trade vehicles with us. He had a big '67 Buick Wildcat, eight cylinder, trailer hitch, and in excellent shape; but he didn't think he would be driving much more. He wondered if we would like his car in place of ours. In spite of knowing the problems with ours, Grandpa

Shatto insisted on the trade. Once more we were overwhelmed at God's supply.

It happened the second time a few years later. We needed a bigger vehicle for our family; and several times, Jerry had passed a SUV-type truck with a "For Sale" sign on it that he wanted to check out. One day, he stopped to talk to the owner; and somehow, on the spur of the moment, Jerry bought it. As soon as he got it home, reality set in. It would need some major interior adjustments to accommodate our family. We would also have to get a trailer hitch put on. But driving up to the pumps was the clincher. We could not believe how much it cost to fill it up—and how often it needed a fill! What had we gotten ourselves into? It was one anxious week as we weighed our options. We decided to take it down to the mechanics shop Jerry's uncles operated to check out getting it converted to propane. When Jerry explained our dilemma, one of his uncles said, "Hey, I know someone who has a crew cab propane truck and really would rather have exactly what you've got there. Why don't you switch with him?" The propane truck was in great shape, already had a trailer hitch, would easily accommodate our family, and even had lots of room to haul all our stuff in the box—we later added a canopy. Best of all, it was economical at the pumps! What a relief! What an answer to our needs! As long as we needed to haul the travel trailer for children's ministry, that truck serviced us well.

In 1987, we again needed to address car concerns. By this time, we had sold the trailer and truck, and our little Datsun hatchback was tight for a family of six. Jerry saw an ad for a second-hand Toyota van. It was three years old with very few miles. The economy and space would be wonderful. But the price, $9,500, was more than we had ever paid for a vehicle. Should we buy it, or should we not? It really did not matter to us whichever God's answer was in the matter. We just wanted to know. We had recently read that verse in Proverbs 16:33, *"the lot is cast into the lap; but the whole disposing thereof is of the Lord."* We knew that God often used the outcome of the Urim and Thummim to reveal His will to the children of Israel. We also knew the story of how the disciples chose between Joseph and Matthias to replace Judas by *"giving forth their lots"* (Acts 1:26). Could we use that method of discerning God's will for us? Regardless of all the theological arguments for or against such a method, we had full confidence that God knew our hearts and could direct the outcome.

We wrote out on slips of paper, "Yes," "No," and "Wait." Then we prayed. We tossed the folded slips on the bed and then drew our answer. It was "Yes!" With some trepidation, we went ahead and purchased the van. For the next 17 years it was our trademark. Well, actually, one time we traded with a man who was leaving Canada, for a year newer Toyota van with fewer miles—plus air conditioning! But it looked just the same.

After 17 years, our kids were tired of that tan van and really wished for a different "look." But that was not really a priority to us. In November 2002, we headed out to the west coast to visit supporters and to take part in a missionary conference. We were thankful for beautiful weather and bare, mountain roads. There was some frost, and we wondered if it was that, or something more sinister, that was causing our van to slip a bit on steep grades. By the time we reached Abbotsford, BC, the diagnosis was clearly "clutch." When we called our kids back home, they were ecstatic! Maybe we could get a different car at last.

We hoped our old faithful van would last a few more days before we needed to make the repairs as we planned to go over to Vancouver Island to make some contacts and visit an uncle, dying with cancer. At the last minute, some supporters graciously loaned their vehicle for a few days. It was an almost new Toyota Corolla—very nice!

On November 7, we took our van in for repair. The estimate was $800 but the service center only charged $570.07 and the van was happy! Our kids weren't! "Boo!" they muttered.

Every evening prior to the missionary conference, we had been unloading the van—all our projection and computer equipment, as well as our display materials—and bringing everything into the house for the night. Then we would load it all up again to take with us to various supporters' houses during the day. The last evening before the conference, when we arrived at our host family's home, we debated about just leaving everything in the van. "After all," Jerry reasoned, "we're going to set up things at the church for the missions' conference first thing in the morning." But contrary to Jerry's preferences, he heeded my advice that night; and we hauled everything in.

Next morning, our host headed off to work, but came back inside to ask us where we had left our van. We thought he was joking. Jerry said, "It's right out there where we parked it." But it wasn't. During the night it had been stolen! Our old van was apparently the vehicle of choice for a joy ride! Why didn't they take it before the clutch repair? When we called our kids back home, their immediate response was "Hooray!" They were hopeful, yet again, about getting a new car! But God wasn't finished with our van.

When we reported it to the police, they already knew where the van was—in the backside of a late model Mazda. Our kids were rather disappointed that the police had found our van, but there was another "Hooray!" when they heard it was crashed into another vehicle! We drove over with our hostess to see what was left, and it looked bad! But when we walked around to see the front of the van, we were amazed! Our van had definitely won the confrontation! The Mazda's back window had served like an air bag as our van had launched right through the back of the Mazda. Not even a headlight was broken! Our Toyota van did have a few interesting new features—like now having only three of its Ford hubcaps remaining, sporting an extra scratch here and there, and featuring an ignition switch that even our house key could turn! The policeman just said, "Have a good drive home." But our kids back in Calgary said, "Double boo!"

As we were heading back across the Rockies, we were overwhelmed with how God had provided. God had amazingly supplied the funds for the trip and for the clutch repair expenses. But when an envelope full of money fell down from Jerry's sun visor as we headed down the road, we felt a little like Joseph's brothers discovering their grain money in their sacks. When we counted the bills, we were now "$500 over costs—and a bit nervous about what was coming next!

The answer came when we got home to find our hot water tank had succumbed to a watery grave. The repair bill was $472.41.

Later, when our automobile insurance company came out to appraise the damage on our van, the appraiser gave us $1,000 compensation. However, we decided that none of the issues really needed to be repaired for our needs! And the kids had to wait a little longer to get a different car!

Then the phone rang on February 21, 2004. It was a call from some supporters at the coast. "We've got some tithe money to give from an inheritance and we're thinking about sending $10,000 in to your ministry for projects, plus an additional $5,000 to you guys personally towards replacing your vehicle." Wow! What do you say? We clearly explained that if they gave money personally towards our vehicle replacement, it could not be receipted as a charitable donation. We suggested they might want to rethink that.

A day later, they called back again. "We've talked it over and felt God wanted us to add to that amount of $5,000 for your vehicle and make it $10,000." The man continued, "We decided we could start saving again towards our holiday trip next year. Oh, and right after we decided to do that, we got the notice of an unexpected bonus from work—$7,100! Isn't God good?"

At last it seemed that our children were going to get their wish. God was about to replace our faithful old tan van. When we finally found a van we thought would be the one for us, we prayed and asked God for confirmation on the price. We told the owner our amount—somewhat lower than her asking price that had already been reduced that week. She said she would have to think about it. After thanking her, we headed to the front door and put on our shoes. Just as we were opening the door, she said, "I've thought about it. You can have it for that amount." Again the thought hit us, "How big is your God!"

Does God care about houses and vehicles too? *"Seek ye first the kingdom of God and His righteousness and all these things shall be added unto you"* (Matthew. 6:33).

EPILOGUE

He asked the question very early in the morning thousands of years ago. King Darius had spent a sleepless night—no food, no music. He could not stand the suspense. What had happened to Daniel? He had to know. It was Darius' pride that had precipitated the crisis. His top ruler, Daniel—or what was left of him—was now at the bottom of the lions' den, thanks to his own ridiculous decree. And Darius, in spite of all his pomp and power, was absolutely helpless to change the course of events.

That morning, Scripture says, when Darius came to the den, he cried with a sad voice, *"Daniel, is your God big enough to deliver you from the lions?"*

And back came Daniel's reply…*"My God IS big enough!"* (Robinson paraphrase).

God was big enough for Daniel, and He certainly has been big enough for us. If anything of lasting value was accomplished in our ministry, it had to be the workings of a big God! We were so small, so very human in our reactions to crises, so inadequate in our expertise, so stumbling in our Christian walk. Yet it was

God that arranged for us to meet at Bible school. It was God that sovereignly dictated the course of our ministry years, that worked in so many lives, and that provided in so many ways. It was God that brought individuals into our lives to mentor us, to pray for us, to encourage and support us. And it was God that used the hard times to pursue us, to show us the ugliness of the self-life and teach us a better way, the way of rest, peace, and victory in Him.

On February 26, 2010 we got an email from Dorothy. She was replying to our spring newsletter sent out just that morning. Dorothy had been a counselor for us years ago at Camp Chestermere while she was attending Prairie Bible College. She now serves as a missionary in Romania with gypsies. Part of her email read as follows:

> Jerry, it was so encouraging to read a situation (in the newsletter) where He so wonderfully worked to make contact with the very people you wanted to talk to, even though you had no idea how to make it happen. It's neat that God has given you the personality, heart, compassion and gift to go and speak to and with young people.
>
> I'll NEVER forget your message in chapel (1983) at PBI: HOW BIG IS YOUR GOD?

Dorothy went on to talk about the potential results of our college recruitment trips for GOM:

> There will be so many encouraging stories in eternity. I can just hear some guy (or gal) coming up

to you in heaven and saying, 'You probably don't remember me, but you spoke at our Missionary Conference... God really touched and challenged my heart to go overseas through something you said when we talked. I ended up having the privilege of serving Him in many countries and seeing Him do great and mighty things to His praise and glory...I wanted you to know that your visit wasn't in vain.'

That would be great if someone was so impacted! But God did not say, "It is required in stewards, that a man be found successful, or talented, or accomplished, or popular, or all the things we look for in greatness." He said in 1 Corinthians 4:2, *"It is required in stewards, that a man be found faithful."* At the end of each day, we only need to hear His "Well done!" That is a great encouragement.

Even now, as we look back over so many events, we catch glimpses of the beautiful tapestry that God was designing. Lessons and experiences from one stage of life were just what we needed for the next chapter. People we touched in early ministry have emerged in later years to come alongside us. Individuals whose lives were transformed in the past have gone into the business of reaching and discipling others.

And what is next? New opportunities? Change? New aches and pains? Loss? Less energy? An uncertain world with huge needs? Still we are challenged with finishing well, and making each day count. And as we look forward to the next chapters of life, however our story unfolds, we must affirm, like Daniel, "Our God is big enough!"

P.S.

The Funny Stuff

Cleaning the overhead projector on a Monday afternoon started out as a good idea. We were scheduled for a children's meeting that night, the first of a weeklong Kids Krusade. Since our overhead projector had last been used out at camp, it was due for a good cleaning. There was dust under the glass. Jerry is very handy and has no fear of taking things apart to fix them. It has been a wonderful blessing over the years—most of the time. Sometimes it was anything but! This turned out to be one of the latter.

There were two logical places to work on such projects—the kitchen table, or the living room floor. This one was happening on the big braided rug in our apartment living room. Everything was going well until Jerry dismantled something, only to discover that it was spring loaded. Sure enough, the springs went flying. But on the variegated colors and textures of the rug, those little springs were a challenge to find. Jerry was on his hands and knees, diligently searching, and searching, and searching!

Three springs were finally located, but the fourth was nowhere to be found.

Meanwhile, I was in our little apartment kitchen, getting things lined up for supper, and listening to the increasing levels of frustration. Finally, it erupted. "Connie, get in here and help me find that spring!"

This was no time to debate the issue. Quickly, I dropped what I was doing and headed to the living room. I took one look at Jerry and began to laugh. That made the situation even worse. Now he was furious! Not only was he unable to find the spring, but his wife was just standing there laughing at him. And he had to get that machine back together soon!

The more frustrated he got, the harder I laughed. He shouted, "Don't just stand there; get looking for it!" But I didn't need to! I had already found it. The missing spring was dangling from his hair; and the more he sputtered, the more the spring bobbled up and down. It was really quite hilarious!

He did eventually get the overhead projector back together—shiny clean. And I didn't get divorced!

It really is true! I try to obey the laws of the land, even when no one is around. I wait for the pedestrian crosswalk light before crossing, whether cars are coming or not. And I signal to change lanes even when I am the only driver for miles around. It goes against my grain to do otherwise. But Jerry tends to be more practical. At least that is what he would call it. And on one terribly rainy day, I thought he had a point—for a bit.

We were on our way to the west coast. It was dark and stormy, and Jerry was totally focused on trying to see where he was driving with the windshield wipers swishing back and forth at top speed. I was in the back seat, struggling with Jeremy. He was just a little guy at that time, but had a very big mess in his diaper. In fact, it was full-blown diarrhea—terribly powerful stuff! We used our more economical cloth diapers at home; but on the road, we often opted for disposables. I set to work to get Jeremy cleaned up. Since seat belt legislation was not in place back then, it made the job legal at least.

At last, Jeremy was taken care of and back into his car seat; but there was an ongoing aroma from the very dirty diaper. It had borderline gag propensities! Jerry was desperately trying to watch for a wayside garbage disposal, but mile after mile, there was nothing to be found. It was no wonder he couldn't locate one. He could barely see the road in front of him, let alone any wayside scenery. All the time, the deadly aroma was ripening— doubling in potency every few minutes, or so it seemed.

Finally Jerry had had enough. "Roll down the window and throw that thing out!" he ordered.

Now I knew that littering was wrong, but I also knew that disobeying your husband was wrong—both backed up by scriptural principles! I didn't take time to sort out all the theological priorities at that point. One thing I did know was that my failure to obey promptly could result in dire consequences—death by asphyxiation, by car accident, or by murder—mine!

I decided to obey. I rolled down the side window, and flung the offending diaper up and out so it would not smear all along the car on its way to a new location. Ahhhh! What a relief to be free of that wretched smell.

I expected Jerry to make some affirming comments from the front seat, some word of praise or approval. After all, I had just done the unthinkable—for me, that is! But he was strangely silent. It didn't take long for me to catch on. His complete attention was fixed on the rear view mirror at car behind that was trying to pass us. The driver had to be crazy—passing in that weather! Jerry pulled to the right, as much as possible, to give the car more space.

As the car pulled alongside us, we glanced over—and couldn't believe our eyes! There was a strange white object attached to the passenger windshield wipers, swishing back and forth, back and forth. Yes, it was Jeremy's dirty diaper thoroughly smearing the car's windshield.

We were dumbfounded, dismayed, and doubled over with laughter. The only thing we could do was to slow down dramatically and let the car pass us. And we prayed that we wouldn't meet the driver at the next gas station!

Already late because of a forgotten time change, Jerry had changed quickly and hurried off for his weekly evening of badminton with some church friends. It was a mixed group of all ages, including a former employer, Jeremy's kindergarten teacher, and some close friends. Upon arrival, Jerry was immediately invited to play on the farthest court with some church missionaries. Hurrying, he slipped off his jeans, grabbed his racket, and headed over to play.

After some warm-up practice, they began their game. The score was 2 to 5, and it was Jerry's turn to serve. He looked down at the birdie in his hand and suddenly realized he was standing there in his underwear—his Stanfield's specials—and not the boxer variety, I'm afraid! He was absolutely stunned. He had forgotten to put his gym shorts on under his jeans in his haste to leave home! However, knowing it was too late for a graceful exit, and realizing he would never live this down as it was, he made a spur-of-the-moment decision to bluff it. He kept on playing, underwear and all.

That whole evening, he pretended nothing was amiss, in spite of the curious glances and muffled laughter. During one game, there were two ladies playing against him named Mrs. Bunn and Mrs. Comfort. They began giggling; and right in the middle of the game, they stopped playing and just stood there holding each other, laughing. They said, "Jerry, you don't know why we're laughing do you?"

He answered, "No, why *are* you laughing?" They just shook their heads, too embarrassed to tell him the truth.

Each time he caught someone chuckling at him, he would smile back innocently, leaving the person feeling helpless. How could anyone get Jerry to catch on? Some of the wives would motion to their husbands to go and tell him, but the men just shook their heads. Finally, one friend named Bob Butt sat down on the bench beside Jerry during a break. Bob slapped Jerry's leg and said, "How are you tonight?"

Jerry slapped Bob's knee right back and said, "Just fine!" Even Bob didn't know what to say. Absolutely no one had the courage to speak up! No one was brave enough to tell Jerry of his obviously inappropriate attire, and so no one could openly enjoy his blunder.

On the way home that night, Jerry could hardly believe what he had done. When he got in the door, he said, "Honey, you'd better sit down."

When I heard his story, my first words were, "Which pair were you wearing?" He had some shorts that were more presentable than others. Then I began to shake my head. "You didn't!" I said. "Tell me you didn't!"

Shortly after this event, some friends from Abbotsford began telling us this crazy story they had heard about someone playing badminton the whole night in his underwear with the Butts, the Bunns, and the Comforts. Jerry didn't let on immediately that he was the unfortunate main character of that story. But we were sure amazed at how fast news travels!

Since that day, he has been asked on many occasions to tell his "short" story.

Years later, Jerry had been up at Peace River Bible Institute (PRBI) doing some recruiting. A few days after he got back, he finally worked up enough courage to tell me another "short" story. On the way up to PRBI, he had stopped to spend the night with a couple that had faithfully supported us for many years. Years ago, Rod had been one of our counselors at Camp Chestermere. He worked diligently with the horses, but he had needed a lot of refining in life. It was amazing to see how he had grown over the years. He and his wife were active in their church. Rod was part of the leadership, taught Sunday School and even preached sometimes.

Rod had married a veterinarian, but she gave up her job to work with Rod in his business of crafting custom-made saddle trees, the inner part of a horse saddle. They could choose where they wanted to locate for a business like that, so their remote, rural home in northern Alberta suited them just fine. Some nights, the northern lights were awesome from their porch. But usually at night it was pretty dark out there.

They had just built a new home on their property, and what a joy to see them in a house with more room. They even had a guest room now—across the hall and down a bit.

They usually got up early, so they had already gone to bed when Jerry finished showering. He folded his towel and left it on the counter to the right as you enter the main bathroom. Since there was an ensuite with the master bedroom, he had this bathroom to himself.

As he went down the hall to his room, he noticed that the door was shut to their bedroom. Jerry quietly went into his room across the hall, but left the door ajar just a little to allow the heat to circulate. After doing some reading, he turned off the light.

It was about 3:00 a.m. that Jerry woke up and realized he needed to make a little trip across the hall. There was one problem. It was dark—so dark you could not see your hand in front of your face. But that was a good thing because, as previously mentioned, Jerry does not own pajamas. With it being so dark, he would not even need to pull on his jeans.

As quietly as possible, Jerry got up and began to feel his way to the door. Yes, his hands felt the dresser shape, and then there was the doorframe. He was doing well. When he got into the hallway, he still could not make out a thing. He began to shuffle down the hall, feeling for the bathroom doorway. There it was. Silently he took a few steps inside.

Now he remembered his towel—he had left it on the counter. His hands started to feel up and down, up and down as he inched his way along. Where was that towel? Maybe it was further in than he thought. He figured he should almost be to the toilet by now. Suddenly, on one of his downward sweeps, he finally felt it. The towel! But just as suddenly, a deep voice said, "Yeeees?"

Jerry stopped dead in his tracks. He knew from the night before that the sounds carried very well from their bathroom into his. They must be awake, too, in the next room.

He felt again for the towel. Again the voice said, "Yeeees, can I help you?"

It was a moment of sheer terror. Jerry finally realized he was really in the master bedroom! Amazingly he had missed bumping into the furniture. In fact, he had managed to shuffle all the way to the far end of the bed and was actually patting Rod's feet. Jerry did not say a word. He was too shocked. He sincerely hoped Rod would not turn on the light, as he was standing there rather exposed. If he thought he had to go to the bathroom before, he really had to go now! As silently as he could, Jerry inched back the way he came, and this time went further down the hall—into the right room!

He had just crawled back into bed when he heard someone up, and saw a flashlight tracing all up and down his doorway. Then he heard Rod go on down the hall, checking the bathroom, and then on out into the main area before returning to his room.

In the morning, Jerry heard Rod up making breakfast for himself, so Jerry went out to join him. Something had to be said. Jerry asked Rod how his night had been. "Oh, good," said Rod. "But have you ever felt there was something or somebody in your room?" Rod went on to explain how he sensed *something* in his room, and that *something* had touched his feet. But when he said, "Yes, can I help you?" nobody answered. He decided to get up and check out the house, just in case the dog got out of his kennel and was putting his paws on the bed. After checking everything and finding nothing amiss, he had just gone back to bed.

Jerry sheepishly had to confess what happened.

Rod began to laugh. He said," You're just lucky you touched my feet and not my wife's! She would have hit the ceiling." And then he made a comment about the gun he kept beside the bed! Yikes!

I would bet Rod has a night-light in the hallway for our next visit!

It was the first time I had met Bob Toews. Jerry had invited him and his wife to spend the night with us before heading back home to Winnipeg. They were mission representatives and Jerry had visited with them at several Bible college conferences. Bob's wife had attended Berean Bible College years ago, so we had a few things in common as well.

We had a good time visiting. We even talked about serious doctrinal issues—like, will all our clothes be left behind when the rapture takes place? Ha! Then the men went on to more interesting matters—tales of Bible school days and some of the pranks they had done.

The question was asked about how I ever got connected with Jerry. They couldn't imagine me ever doing such things. Jerry said, "Oh, you just don't know what she's really like." Two stories came out.

The first happened when Brett and Jaclyn were dating. Brett accidentally left his backpack at our place. I checked through it to make sure there was nothing urgent for that day's classes. In the process, I found a nice T-shirt. I turned it inside out, carefully stitched the armholes shut, and then turned it right side out again. I also put a container of freshly baked cookies in the backpack before delivering it to his college. The next day he called, very politely thanking me for the wonderful cookies and for delivering his backpack.

It was not till several days later that he grabbed that shirt and put it on—or at least tried to. He stuck his arms up and…"Hey! What's with this thing?" He couldn't find the armhole openings. What had happened? He couldn't think when or how his shirt had been pranked, or who would have done such a thing. Jaclyn said she was innocent, and he never dreamed it would be me!

The second story took place when Jordan and Julie were dating and they came for a visit from Prairie Bible College. They often did laundry while they were here; and one time, Jordan happened to leave a pair of black boxer shorts. Perfect! I got some pink embroidery thread and stitched a design on the backside—a heart with the words, "Cutie pie" inside. The next time the Prairie basketball teams were playing in Calgary, Jerry and I went to watch. Jordan and Julie were both captains of their teams. I observed carefully where Jordan's gym bag was—a difficult task as the bags were all alike. When the guys went off for a break, I carefully returned the boxer shorts to his bag, with the embroidered design discreetly folded inside. You can imagine the ridicule from his teammates when those came out!

Our overnight guests were a little surprised that I would actually be involved in such treachery! After some more visiting and laughter with our company, we all turned in for the night.

The next morning after our company left, I was changing the bed. Lo and behold, there was a pair of shorts left behind. I couldn't believe my eyes. And then I began to chuckle. This was too perfect an opportunity to pass up—especially in light of the stories from the night before! After doing the laundry, I set to work. What could be more appropriate than to embroider the words *"Left behind"* on the left backside of the shorts! After all, it seemed perfectly fitting. It was the *left behind* of the shorts, the shorts were *left behind*, and if the rapture had taken place, perhaps the garment would have been *left behind* as well, although there is room for more theological debate on that score! We carefully wrapped them up, put a little note inside, and clearly marked the outside of the package "Confidential." We only had the mission office address in Winnipeg, so that is where the package was sent.

For months we didn't hear a thing. I hoped I hadn't offended our guests. After all, I had only met Bob once. Then Jerry ran into them, at another college missionary conference and they began to laugh. I guess the whole Winnipeg office staff had been curious about this "Confidential" package that came in the mail for Bob; and when he opened it in front of them all and read the note, the laugh was on him. I am afraid, however, that I'm losing my reputation for being "prim and proper!"

Our home seems to have a steady stream of overnight guests; and maybe, sometime in the future, it will be your turn. Just be careful not to leave any articles of clothing behind!